GOD'S
FINGERPRINTS

GOD'S
FINGERPRINTS

IMPRESSIONS OF NEAR
DEATH EXPERIENCES

EDITED BY
JODY LONG

www.whitecrowbooks.com

God's Fingerprints

Impressions of Near Death Experiences

Published and printed in the United States of America and the United Kingdom
by White Crow Books; an imprint of White Crow Productions Ltd.

For information, contact White Crow Books
at 3 Merrow Grange, Guildford, GU1 2QW United Kingdom,
or e-mail to info@whitecrowbooks.com.

Cover Designed by Butterflyeffect
Interior design by Velin@Perseus-Design.com

Paperback ISBN 978-1-910121-05-4
eBook   ISBN 978-1-910121-06-1

Non Fiction / Body, Mind & Spirit / Mysticism

www.whitecrowbooks.com

CONTENTS

NDERF

The Near Death Experiencer Research Foundation (NDERF) has humble beginnings from 1998 at a time when the internet and websites were dubious at best. Destiny intervened when near-death experience researcher Jeffrey Long, MD was able to get information directly from the near death experiencers. The site became a tool to gather NDE data. As the internet became more widespread, so did the global outreach of being able to share information. Now, the NDE accounts come from every corner of the world, from every walk of life, and all ages. The only limitation to this data is that the experiencers have to be able to use a computer or know someone who can use a computer on their behalf.

I became webmaster in 2002, gave the website a facelift, started the global outreach project, and have been providing website and e-mail support for NDErs and world since that time. We have over 500,000 hits per month from 183 out of the 195 countries all over the world. Additionally, over 500 volunteers translate the website into over 23 languages. Since Evidence of the Afterlife was published in 2010, the website has grown exponentially. We have also helped countless big television networks, authors, magazines, and students to understand and produce positive research, presentations, films, documentaries, and other media outreach on NDEs.

www.nderf.org

FOREWORD

My grandmother died in February 2010. My grandfather and she had been together for over 75 years. Yes, that's right — my grandfather is 95 years old and still alive. He was pretty devastated when grandma passed over and felt like a part of him died that month.

Much to my surprise, my grandfather admitted to me that he had several after death communications (ADCs) from her. He said he could feel her presence, she appeared in dreams, and sometimes she talked to him. He also told me that he was interested in the near death experience (NDE) and would like to read some of the experiences. So, I copied over 500 pages in large print so he could see it, put it into a couple of 4" D-ring binders, and sent them to him.

What started as a kernel of an idea - to make reading NDEs more accessible to those who don't have access to a computer, germinated so everyone can read a book of these precious outcrops containing stories of love and hope.

INTRODUCTION

WHAT IS A NDE?

What is a NDE and why would you care? The first part is easy to answer. It is when a person dies or has an imminently life threatening event and then has an experience during the time of death or unconsciousness. Then the person is resuscitated and comes back to tell of the experience.

There are certain characteristics of a NDE, but not everyone experiences all of these elements during their event. Characteristics of NDE includes the OBE, tunnel, light at the end of the tunnel, beautiful surroundings or scenery, spiritual guides, deceased loved ones, other beings, life review, universal knowledge, oneness, unconditional love, decision to return to the body, and consciousness in the body again.

Interestingly, there appears to be a certain order to the elements. That means that even though many experiencers report that there is no time on the other side or that time doesn't happen like here on earth, there is a sequence to the events. For instance, the out of body experience (OBE) doesn't happen at the end of the experience. The awareness of being out of body happens at the beginning of the experience. Another example concerns the decision to return to the body. Once the decision is made or at the end of the experience, the NDEr usually comes back to their body fairly quickly. It is rare that someone is told they are coming back to earth and yet, they stay to see other things in the afterlife.

WHAT HAPPENS DURING A NDE?

The beginnings of a NDE are more like an out of body experience (OBE) where experiencers can see, hear, and move around in our physical plane, but they can't usually be seen by other people in this three dimensional reality. Many people would equate this to being a ghost.

Usually during NDEs, experiencers tell us they perceive the universal matrix soon after their "consciousness" leaves the body. The environment includes feelings and knowledge of unconditional love, total universal knowledge, telepathy, interconnectedness, and oneness. I like to call it the universal matrix because the feelings experienced in this particular state of being appears to be what makes up the other side. This stage is what we perceive and the backdrop to how we operate as a conscious being outside of our physical body.

The tunnel has many different descriptions and is technically not part of the elements of the formal NDE studies. However, there are so many people that describe the tunnel, that I call it an element. The tunnel can have color, the sense of motion (like being in a vortex, moving fast, or going up or down), and it usually has a light at the end of it that gets larger towards the end of the tunnel. A guide, relative, or being may accompany the person through the tunnel.

On the other side of the tunnel or while going through the tunnel, a person sometimes experiences a life review. The life review can be of this life or include other lives. While there are many descriptions of how a person can see their life, such as in spherical vision or flashing before their eyes, there are two main features of a life review. Typically, the person is the only one who judges themself. The other feature of the life review is that it isn't just a memory of what happened to the NDEr. The NDEr can perceive the action through the eyes of others. It is a ripple of cause and effect whereby every action they took on earth is perceived through the emotions of another person as a reaction to the experiencer's initial action. For instance, the NDEr would feel how their angry words affected the person the anger was directed at. They would feel the other person's pained reaction. Consequently, because of judging one's self and understanding the effects of their earthly actions, the life review is credited as a major reason why NDErs make changes in their life. Post NDE, they tend to be more loving in their interactions with others on earth.

After the tunnel, there is usually beautiful scenery or a warm, loving light. Experiencers report scenery as diverse as rolling hills to crystal castles, and everything in between. Many times the plants and the water will have a vibrancy, color, and sound not known here on earth. A person moves through this scenery by thought and often times perceives this as floating. You rarely hear someone say they walked somewhere in this beautiful place.

The beings that NDErs report meeting the most are deceased relatives. This has been a finding and part of the formal NDE studies since the 1970s. However, unreported and from the NDERF research data is that most of these deceased relatives are blood relatives. On the other hand, it is not uncommon for NDErs to be guided or reunited with spouses or significant others. I suspect that there would be more reports of deceased spouses or significant others in NDEs except that it would tend to make the NDErs not want to come back to their body!

The decision to come back may or may not be up to the NDEr. Often times, there is a greeter who tells the experiencer that it is not their time yet. Those who are given a choice on whether to come back or not, will come back either because they need to complete learning lessons on earth or they choose to come back to raise their children. Reentry into the body can sometimes be difficult. I have heard it described in terms of "jarring" or like being squished into a tube of toothpaste.

After the NDEr comes back, it usually takes them 7 years to integrate their experience into their earthly life. For the most part, many NDErs report they are angry at being back because they didn't want to leave paradise and that they long to return "home"; which intriguingly implies that this earth is not our true home.

Part of the integration process has to do with telling the story of their experience. Many times the NDE is ineffable because there are no earthly words to explain what happened on the other side. It is a lot like trying to explain the color red to a blind person. So, the NDEr has to order what they experienced and then explain their experience in a way that makes sense to others. Many will use analogies like there was so much love it "felt like love times a million." Or the sun was so bright, but it didn't hurt my eyes. And still others report that even though they can analogize to something we know on earth, they still can't adequately explain what they experienced.

Additionally, part of the integration process is coming to terms with the reality of what they experienced on the other side and comparing it to the reality of earth. When a person experiences total, 100% unconditional love and then comes back to earth, it is a real shock to their system. It is easy to understand why they would be angry at returning to earth. On the other hand, those who understand that they have a mission to do or a lesson to learn, seem to do better with the fact that they returned to earth.

The core behavior changes happen because of the integration process of trying to come to terms with they experienced over there and the fact that it is so different than what we find on earth. Many of the old paradigms, such as bad relationships or ego-based behavior (like materiality) are changed because the NDEr is trying to become more like what they experienced on the other side. NDErs become much more loving, compassionate, forgiving, patient, more tolerant, less judgmental, more helpful to others, and less materialistic.

Many people are curious about hellish NDEs. There are some NDEs that are not pleasant or heavenly. In fact, some are downright hellish. But the good news is that these experiences are relatively rare. In Barbara Rommer's book, *Blessings in Disguise* she detailed different types of less than positive NDEs. Among these were the void and the hellish experience. Some of the frightening NDEs, such as the void, have to do with how the experience was perceived. We have many void experiences where people really enjoy the warm, dark, womb-like void. We also have several void experiences where the person is afraid of being alone in the nothing-ness. We have one person who was afraid of angels and was trying to bat them away because he didn't want to be dead. To him, angels were terrifying while most experiencers were comforted by their presence. We also have several NDEs that started in hell or they visited hell and then they ended in heaven. Consequently, labels such as "less than positive" or "hellish" are relative. These types of experiences can also have a silver lining because many people will correct their behavior when they return to earth in order to mitigate any unpleasant outcomes on the other side.

Yes, there is a hell. But it is different than what many religions teach. According to the NDErs, it isn't an eternal place of damnation. Rather it is a personal hell that experiencers have a choice to come out of and go to their place in heaven. NDEr George Ritchie explained that each person in hell had an angel watching over them. All those people had to do was to look up.

I also know of one person who went to hell as a test of his character. Ultimately, he chose self-annihilation rather than to be a part of evil. This was like a baptism of fire to purify his soul. His experience is the exception though.

After over a decade of studying NDEs, I've observed a less than positive NDE may help experiencers to change their path on earth. Even the positive or heavenly NDEs usually have a drastic impact on the experiencer. I think that the heavenly NDEs either help or changes their experiencer's spiritual path.

One of the more unusual effects of the NDE is the effect it has on others. Not only does it change the person who has the near death experience, but it changes those who read them. The lack of fear of death is a remarkable change. It is a liberation for people to start truly LIVING their lives in a loving manner, rather than just living in a manner to avoid eternal punishment. Instead of focusing on the negatives and living in fear, a person is able to live and act out of love. NDEs talk about unconditional love, peace, kindness, and hope. It is a remarkable gift for people to read about these inspirational experiences.

WHY WOULD YOU CARE ABOUT THE STUDY OF NDE?

The answer to the second part of the question posed above, "What is a NDE and why would you care?" has layers of complexities. On one level, if NDEs are real, it changes everything we know about the world from learning our purpose on earth to how to interact lovingly with other people and everything on the planet. It redefines the very nature of consciousness and our understanding of it. On a scientific level, if our essence survives death, then it provides a paradigm shift in the way we perceive our reality and it expands the world we previously knew through only our 5 earthly senses. That means our essence is also multidimensional and greater than our three dimensional reality. On a medical level, it may change how we take care of ourselves and how we deal with end of life issues. On a personal level, it changes how we interact with others and how we learn to love ourselves. On an emotional level, people who have a near death experience (NDErs) experience "love times a million" and the majority lose their fear of death. On a spiritual level, there is evidence of God, Jesus, and the notions of how we are all interconnected throughout the universe. Heaven becomes the norm and not a place we go if we obey certain earthly rules.

ARE NDE'S REAL?

The number one question we get is "Are NDEs real?" I'm here to tell you that after 14 years, I can answer definitively and resoundingly – YES! The NDE is a mechanism where people explore the afterlife and then come back to tell us about it. That's the short answer.

Science cannot explain what causes NDE. I think that at some point, the burden of proof changes when you have 5-15% of the population experience a NDE. Science can't call them ALL hallucinatory or delusional. Moreover, any scientific explanation doesn't get to pick and choose which evidence fits their theory. The hypothesis must fit all the evidence for a theory in order for it to be considered as proof. So instead of saying that NDEs are not real because they can't be proven, the shift in burden of proof is that NDEs are real until proven otherwise.

As a little history, the majority of study of NDEs came in the 1970s when a scientific group of people got together and formed IANDS – the International Association of Near Death Studies. The early work of Raymond Moody, Kenneth Ring, and Bruce Greyson, provided the groundwork for the study of the NDE and also piqued the interest of the public. Since that time, the lack of funding for this area of study is one of the reasons why not much is happening in the world of NDE research.

The race to explain the near death experience has been one of the most sought after "brass rings" in the area of consciousness research. The reason I talk about the brass ring is because the NDE is the strongest evidence for the reality of the afterlife. Therefore, if a scientist can discount the NDE, then they are able to atheistically say there is no God or afterlife. This is a big deal in the scientific community.

The scientist who comes up with evidence that NDEs are caused in the brain or by body chemistry, is celebrated by media and science journals. As such, there has been a whole host of explanations for why NDEs are not real. We have many of the early explanations such as anoxia (lack of oxygen to the brain), the dying brain, brain chemistry, delusions, and hallucinations. Later, the explanations got fancier with random memories, angular gyros, autoscopy, and REM intrusion. Nevertheless, what is interesting about these theories is that none have ever explained the NDE because if it had they wouldn't keep coming up with theories!

For instance, the latest NDE skeptic argument of the week is the rat brain study. The scientists found that there was a spike in brain activity as they killed the rat. The dying process is much different in humans, yet the study suggested that humans are the same as rats without providing any science to back that hypothesis up. When I was dying in the hospital, I don't care if my brain activity spiked or not. I couldn't hold a conscious thought, much less an organized, lucid thought. NDErs always have detailed, organized, hyper-lucid thoughts. Consequently, the Rat Brain study has nothing to do with NDE.

As in Pim von Lommel's study, the spike would have to be predictive and correlative as to who has a NDE and who hasn't. The authors offered their rat study as a way to study NDE. Media turned the study into something it isn't. In order for the rat brain study to be valid for humans, every human who dies would have organized, lucid thoughts based upon spikes in their brain. This is because every rat they tested had spikes of EEG activity in the brain. To suggest that the EEG spike in all the rats causes NDEs, actually tends to disprove the correlation because NDEs only occur in 5-15% of the people who die and are resuscitated rather than happening to everyone.

The Rat Brain study hadn't correlated the findings with a single human, yet the media heavily publicized the study because the term NDE was used. They thought they'd found the skeptic's smoking gun. If scientists had said anything else other than "NDE," the study would never have gotten the publicity. So, I look at this type of scientific write-up as a form of intellectual dishonesty used for personal recognition and future research money.

On the other hand, there are plenty of reasons that are ignored by these scientists. Dr. Jeff Long has detailed nine of these lines of evidence in his book, *Evidence of the Afterlife: the Science of Near Death Experience*. What science or the above theories cannot explain is:

1) Lucid Death (NDErs report increased alertness and consciousness). When the brain is dead or severely compromised such as what happens in a NDE, there is no organized linear thought.

2) Out-of-Body Experiences (NDErs provide evidence from verifiable experiences). Von Lommel reported one of the more striking examples in the Lancet. Apparently, a man had his dentures removed during the time he was coding. He did not see this nurse prior to dying. He saw the nurse put them on a certain shelf. After he was revived, he described the nurse to the staff and told her where she put his dentures.

3) Blind Sight (NDErs blind from birth report a form of "vision" during their NDEs). How is this possible unless they were able to see outside of their physically limited body?

4) Impossibly Conscious (NDErs report experiences while under anesthesia). During anesthesia, a person is unconscious and does not have the same brain function as a normally awake person. This is an extension of the Lucid Death observation in #1) above.

5) Perfect Playback (NDErs report life reviews that include experiencing the feelings of others). Many times, experiencers will see events as they actually happened and that they had long forgotten or remembered differently (inaccurately).

6) Family Reunion (NDErs report seeing dead relatives, including people unknown to them who were identified to them later by viewing family photographs).

7) From the Mouths of Babes (NDErs who are children have every NDE element of older NDErs, and this is true whether the account is told during childhood or from an adult who had the experience in childhood). If the NDE elements were different, then one could say that NDE was by some element of age. But, there is no difference in the content of the NDE, so age cannot account for who will have a NDE or not.

8) Worldwide Consistency (NDErs who are non-English-speakers form the largest collection of cross-cultural NDEs and provide evidence that NDEs are the same all over the world). NDEs are a common, human experience that happens to everyone regardless of age, culture, religious preference, or ethnicity.

And

9) Changed Lives (NDErs report that their lives change because of their NDE, and the majority report a change for the better). The radical change in the core behavior and beliefs of the experiencers is a key component of the NDE. It takes most NDErs and average of 7 years to integrate their experience with their waking reality.

There has been one major prospective study done by Pim von Lommel as the lead researcher. This work was published in the prestigious medical journal the Lancet in 2001. The study involved many different hospitals and started with 344 cardiac patients over a period of 8 years. There were 18% of those patients who had a NDE, while 12%

of the NDEs reported a core experience. A core experience is a deep NDE that has at least a score of 6 of the NDE elements according to the Weighted Score Experience Index scale developed by Kenneth Ring. The conclusion of the von Lommel study was the NDEs are medically inexplicable. That means there is no medical explanation for why some people have a NDE and why others do not have a NDE.

ANSWERS TO SKEPTIC ARGUMENTS

Von Lommel is a cardiac doctor. As such, cardiac patients may or may not be medicated. Of those who are medicated, many are heavily medicated and others are lightly medicated. NDEs could not be predicted based on medication or lack of medication. Consequently, NDE is not caused by body chemistry, also known as oxygen deprivation, drugs, or chemical reactions of the dying mind.

Some patients who have heart attacks have time to be afraid while others do not. Von Lommel showed that whether a person was afraid or not, could not be used to predict who would have a NDE or not. The fear factor or lack thereof showed that NDEs were not psychologically based.

NDEs are not dreams, hallucinations, or delusions. In the NDERF data set, we directly ask whether NDEs are dreamlike in any way. The NDErs know what a dream is and they know what a NDE is. Most were emphatic that NDEs were definitely not a dream. The vividness of the NDE, longevity of the memory as if it occurred yesterday, ease of recall, and orderly sequence of the NDE made it not like a dream.

About five years ago, I was dying in the hospital emergency room. What I thought were aches, pains and chills from the flu, was actually a kidney infection. I was going into shock. As my body was shutting down, I remember distinctly that I couldn't form a cohesive thought. The brain was shutting down. But what I could do was feel base emotion from the base of the brain. I felt extreme sadness, but didn't have the capacity to reason why I felt this emotion. From that time forward, when scientist theorize that the NDE is brain chemistry, random thoughts, or the dying brain, I emphatically disagree with them. There is no way that while I was dying that I was capable of having a delusion, hallucination, or random memory. I certainly wasn't capable of having a vividly, organized, hyper-lucid thought, let alone an entire experience like the NDErs report.

One of the strongest piece of evidence against the NDE being a hallucination or delusion comes from Melvin Morse, a pediatrician, who studied 112 children. He had one girl who needed medication for her condition that caused her to hallucinate. She also experienced a NDE. She told Dr. Morse that her NDE was nothing like what she experienced after taking her medications.

THE NEAR DEATH EXPERIENCE

With the foregoing discussion as a background of what a NDE is, there is no substitute for reading the experiences for yourself. Then you can make up your own mind about the reality of the NDE. You will also notice how good you feel after you read them. There is something very uplifting when reading stories about love, peace, happiness, and life after this life. Several NDErs on NDERF who have had ICU psychosis or hallucinations report that they can clearly tell the difference between both experiences.

Stylistically, you will notice that there is a narrative and then there are questions afterwards. The narrative allows the experiencer to tell the story as they want to tell it. However, often times, there is so much to tell, that the questions help the NDEr remember or expand on certain parts of what they wrote or didn't feel was important enough to mention in the narrative. Most of the time, if the experiencer capitalizes a word or a sentence; I leave it because the emphasis is one of the few tools they have to really tell their story.

ONE

The first story is Amy C. Amy's story is AMAZING! I learn more from each time I read it. The entire story is so full of details and knowledge. Her connection with her guide is so much stronger than ties on earth. She knew this person, which suggests a pre-existence prior to coming to earth. She experiences the extreme love and spiritual knowledge. What happens is that it takes her 7 years to integrate her profound experience with her earthly reality. Also notice the extreme emotion, vividness, and difficulty in finding the words to explain her experience. She learned many things, but her life review was key to helping her to change her life on earth. The NDE changed her perspective of how she viewed things on earth. The changes helped to make her healthier and happier on earth.

AMY C.

Ever since I was age 17, I'd had chronic pain. The doctors said I had "fibromyalgia." My life had become a tortured existence with sleep difficult to come by. I could only sleep fifteen minutes at a time because it was too painful to hold still for longer than that. Then I'd have to move, stretch and massage my muscles in bed. I was constantly tired and in excruciating pain.

My doctor decided to prescribe a medication that worked on pain so that I could finally sleep. The medication was not used for sleep per se. I started out taking one quarter of a pill. I noticed that even the tiniest amount of these painkillers would cause swelling in my nose and then my breathing would become shallow. My body's reaction to the medication was scary and uncomfortable for me, but I was willing to do anything to relieve the intense pain.

I went back to the doctor and let him know that I was having an allergic reaction to the medication. He chuckled and said that my body simply needed to "get used to the meds." He told me that the dose of three pills was so low; it couldn't possibly cause an allergic reaction.

After a week of agonizing pain and no deep sleep, I gave in and decided to trust the doctor's professional advice. I went to bed after taking all three pills. Within minutes, I felt myself begin to go numb. Then the inside of my nasal passages swelled up so I couldn't breathe. I couldn't even open my mouth. I was struggling to get air, but no air came. My entire body felt like it was becoming mummified. I couldn't move of use any of my muscles. I felt suffocated or encased in my own body, like being buried alive, in my body. I couldn't call out for help, and it only took a couple of minutes before the struggle was over.

I felt like a vacuum cleaner with a strong suction was on the top of my head. I also felt an absolute sense of relief. There was no longer a need to breathe, and no feeling as if I were drugged on the medication. I had no sense of my own body but I felt like I was travelling very quickly.

During my NDE on the other side, people talked telepathically. That means we communicated without actual verbal words. I never heard auditory SOUND, like on earth. People would just look at each other, and even though there were some mouth movements, I would receive the message mind to mind. The messages would come through so quickly, without any effort, from the inside, rather than outside of self. There were very few technically precise words. So, when I quote communications here, I am offering the closest thing to what I understood telepathically.

The next thing I remember is moving through some kind of a portal along with many other beings. It felt like I was in some kind of a waiting room. I was curious and began to watch the others who were coming through the portal. I watched a group of three teenage boys come in. I noticed their abrasive energy. As I was looking at them, it came to me that they had died in a car accident. They had been drinking alcohol.

Another woman came through the portal. She looked like she was in her fifties. She noticed me watching her and took that opportunity to communicate. She was quite the chatterbox. I listened to her for a short while as she told me how proud she was of her body and how well she had taken care of herself in her life. She went on about how good she looked and then she tried to show me her body. I noticed that she had an odd-looking hue to her skin, as if she'd either been going to tanning booths or sunning herself too long. Her hair was an artificial-looking bleached-blonde color. I then understood that she had died of skin cancer. She seemed to want to talk about herself a lot and I became bored. So, I went back to watching the people coming through the portal.

Next, there was a young woman who came up to me. She had beautiful, almost greenish eyes, and the loveliest shade of reddish hair. She was around age 19 or 20. She began to tell me about herself. She told me that she had died slowly blacking out with no way to breathe. It was a feeling like she was drowning, and yet, I wasn't sure she actually had drowned. While she telepathically told me of her death, I actually experienced at a certain level, what she felt. It was as if I was there with her at the time of death.

She started to give me orders, "Tell them this... etc." "Tell them that, etc." She was giving me personal information about herself. I had no idea why, but I politely listened. One thing she said was that she wanted me to "Tell them that I loved to sing." With her beautiful voice, she gave a quick, impromptu singing performance for those immediately around us. I was also awed by how she was free during her performance to actually elevate herself and move through the space around her without touching the ground. It was like watching an underwater dance without the water. I don't know why I wasn't more shocked, or why I accepted this so well. I also noticed how at a certain part of her song, her beautiful red hair seemed to grow longer! I thought how interesting that she could choose to have longer hair at will. After her performance, this young woman continued talking. She told me that she had regretted not "hanging in there." How it "would have been better to stay" and work out her issues and continue learning. But, she wanted me to, "Tell them how free I feel now."

A lot of others came through. I didn't feel the people were either good or bad. It felt like a room of normal people, all unique unto themselves. This place was like a room or an area, but did not feel very bright to me. Somehow, I was receiving information that these people were dead, yet I hadn't fully accepted they were dead because everything felt so real and natural. There was nothing that felt shocking or strange. Everything was so alive!

Then I noticed we had congregated into a much bigger and brighter room or area where there were many, many others present. Everyone was so busy talking and getting to know each other. It felt similar to a scene in a high school cafeteria. People wanted to quickly find others who they were related to or felt at ease with, and there were even little groups that began to form.

After a while, I noticed a Latino man move into the room. I sensed something about him. He felt safe and balanced to me. I knew that I could trust him to tell me what was going on. It still had not occurred to me that I might be dead. As I wondered, "Who are you?" I moved toward him, just by focusing my attention on him. It wasn't like walking on earth. He looked at me and I realized he was a "teacher" or a "guide" for this group. He explained that he had been a truck driver who had died in a truck accident. He told me that he was not a perfect man, but that he had mastered "humility." I could feel truly, that he hadn't a shred of self-regard or egotistic pride, about him. He explained that he had come to help teach the importance of humility to this group of people. They had been self-absorbed in their lives, to such a degree where this had blocked their own vision and spiritual progression. They hadn't been able to learn vital lessons and had aborted their own lives, unwittingly for all I knew. He seemed to be telling me that in one way or another, these people had committed suicide.

I was a bit confused by how the term, "suicide" could come to me with these people. This made me wonder, because I hadn't noticed anyone in the room who had hung themselves, intentionally overdosed on drugs, shot themselves, or things like that. Then, I came to understand that the casual disregard for life, or flagrant and selfish risks that one might take, whether involved in drug use, drunk driving, or any kind of action that could essentially lead to one's own demise is considered like suicide there.

There is also another type of suicide that is different than risk-taking or flagrant disregard of the body. There are other situations when a human takes their own life in desperation, due to emotional or mental imbalances, physical agony, or severe depression. Another example is when a very old person gets so tired of hanging on to their earthly life, that they will themselves to go by simply not eating or breathing. These choices are not punished on the Other Side. (I never witnessed punishment or condemnation FOR ANYTHING). It is considered that the human is willing himself or herself out of this life cycle.

4

The teacher continued to offer more information. These people would have a rest period. He explained how he needed to teach this group of people how vital it is to lose their obsession or fixation with themselves. That they will become stagnant in all spiritual progress if they cannot unchain themselves from their own ankles.

He said there are lessons these people chose to learn. He explained how by aborting their own lives, learning what they needed to learn would be more difficult. I came to understand that as much as they were taught and infused with good and helpful information there, it is one thing to learn theory; it is another to understand the lesson by practicing it. Even if these people agreed wholeheartedly with what was being taught, or what they needed to learn, learning on earth is easier than learning here. He explained that learning their lessons here without a body is like learning to get over an addiction to drugs with no opportunity to do the drugs, or like learning to love one's own enemy without having enemies to deal with.

He had to teach them the importance of humility. And yet, he shook his head, smiling slightly, and implied that there was still very little he could help them with, without their bodies. His service was to help instill more of a passion for what he had to teach. A passion that is strong enough that it would leave a seed of Light that might stay with them through their sojourn.

When this particular teacher was transmitting information to me, I felt a jolt of sudden anxiety and I queried, "What are these people?" He came in more clearly, stating telepathically, "They are deceased. They have died." I remember demanding point blank, "If these people are dead, what am I?" I don't know why it took me so long to grasp the fact of this reality. But then again, time wasn't as it is here, so I am not sure it was "long". He explained gently, "You are in between. You are as if in a coma. There will still be life in you. You are not the same."

With that, I started upward. I wanted out of there. As I moved toward the corner of the room to leave, at least a couple of the teenage boys suddenly lunged at me with an energy like, "She's alive. Touch her!" They were reaching toward me and trying to pull me back toward them. It seemed almost as if they desired sexual contact or energy. This, of course, made me even more determined to leave.

I am not sure if the following took place before, after, or simultaneously with what I just shared. For the sake of some level of written chronology, I express as, "next", "after" or, "then". It could be in that order, but know that I am often tempted to say that it was "all at once."

I then began to move more quickly upward, and I felt that I was safe and comfortable. I was enveloped in Love. There was someone tending to me, and I seemed to be at absolute peace with this Guide. There was so much light coming from his face. Even so, I felt a very maternal sense - it was as if he were like a mother to me. So, I hesitate to label him with a gender. I will refer to this Guide as male, to make things easier for writing purposes.

My vibration was changing. I could feel a big change in frequency, as if I was tuning into a different radio station on a universal grand scale. I was out in the Universe, and I was given a show. It was like having an astronomy teacher speak on the beauty of the Universe while lying under the stars at night. I was out there amidst the stars rather than under them. I remember that during this scene, I saw something like holographic words and numbers move in front of me and past the stars.

It felt like I was downloading information. It was more about receiving information, than visuals and literal details that I can put into clear words. I felt at that time that I understood EVERYTHING. I felt the full truth of Laws and Order in the Universe. One thing that I really remember vividly was the beautiful math of the Universe. I remember understanding that there was a supreme and perfect kind of math that was in and of ALL things. I remember being told something about Einstein! I was so excited. It was such a pleasant experience.

I was also shown how there is a kind of clock-work in the sky. How the stars themselves actually hold a sort of map or mathematical Key to everything that is! "You are written in the stars," I was told! EVERYTHING is! I recall how thrilling this part of my NDE was for me. I wish I had better articulation to describe how wondrous this part was. I was also told that this map in the stars, or the keys that are hidden there, have been known for a long time by many. These things have been sorely corrupted and turned into things of ill or trivial purpose in most cases on our planet, BUT THAT ALL MATTERS SUCH AS THESE SHOULD RETURN TO A MORE SPIRITUAL NATURE.

During my NDE, I came to understand that most of us have lived many times before, MUCH longer than we could even fathom. That our lives that feel so very long are infinitesimal when placed in the whole picture, which for that matter, cannot even be framed. I was shown how every single individual through their own free will chooses paths that mathematically take them to the circumstances of their next existence or life. I learned that nothing at all sits in accident or chaos; that every single aspect of our lives is ruled by natural Laws that we placed OURSELVES in! In a sense, we create our own worlds.

I was shown how one can never assume that if someone lives a life of suffering that this is because of "evil" deeds. Many may choose a life of suffering because of what it Awakens in them, or because of how they can touch others from that position, etc. We can NEVER EVER assume that we can be accurate in guessing why each Being lives the life they live. I cannot describe the relief... the refreshing, peaceful balm this Knowledge was for me. To finally gather the Truth that I'd yearned for all of my life. That all really IS Good! There IS sense and beauty all around. No one is just free-falling as it had seemed before!

God doesn't just get to toy with us as He pleases with random ideas of tests such as rewards and punishments doled out upon His current mood or mindset. Because even who God is, is within those universal Laws. On earth, I had lived in fear, distrust, and panic for 30 consecutive years. While in this experience, out in the vast expanse of stars, planets, moons, and Intelligence, I Knew complete trust for what felt like the first time. This was inexplicable bliss for me. And I remember radiating with gratitude.

I was then brought before what appeared to be a living picture of our planet. While I was looking at it, I saw a word above it. I believe it was "NOVATA". It looked to be one eye opening up. Then the whole planet seemed to open up, like an eyelid that slowly awakens to dawn. There was a lovely, soft woman's voice that spoke the days of the week in a different language, and then said, "Prepare for the Seventh Day." At this, I saw the curious visual of a piano. There was something about music and octaves.

The next thing I remember is traveling quickly over the Earth. It felt very surreal, like I was being shown a movie, and yet the movie seemed alive. It was like an amusement park ride, flying over a panoramic film of a live scene on earth. There were fields of crops all over the earth. As I would zoom in and get closer to the earth, for instance to a field of wheat, I would be told, "This has been poisoned. The food has been altered and poisoned. It is no longer pure. The people are consuming impure food. This is death." I felt sad and concerned about this and wondered why or how it was possible. How could a field of wheat or corn be "poisoned", and WHY?! I was told that man should return to the Earth or death would ensue everywhere. It was said repeatedly during this scene to "Return to the Earth." I was told that upon my return, that I should look for pure food, unadulterated food, and only consume that which is "clean." I dismissed this somewhat, because I had no intention of returning to earth.

Again, it is difficult for me to place any of this in chronological order, as time felt so different there. It was almost as if many things happened at once, and yet, separately.

My Guide lovingly stayed as my support while I had a kind of life review. I never felt chastised at all, even though I know I've been very cruel at times and have hurt many people. I've lost my temper in horrible ways because I had one of the hottest tempers I know of. I have had great trouble with the concept of forgiveness, and yet, I felt only Love and understanding through the entire life review. It felt like I was being given the opportunity and Gift of being able to stand back and more fully understand and love myself. I was able to feel exactly what others around me had felt during my life. I understood how everything I did, said, and thought, had touched others around me in one way or another. I was able to enter the minds and emotional centers of many who had been around me, and understand where they were coming from in their own thinking. I could see how their own personal views and life experiences had shaped their lives. I felt their struggling and their fears, their own desperate need for love and approval, their confusion, and more than anything, I could feel how child-like everyone was. With every person I viewed, including myself, I was able to See and Feel with a Higher Mind and Eye. And the feeling I had toward everyone was nothing less than what a loving mother would feel for her own children at toddler age.

Moments were actually comical. There are beings who are Helpers on the Other Side who have Mastered themselves in many or all ways, and help work with us. I call them the "Elders." They see us and lovingly find so much humor in the way we do things. It might seem brutally annoying to consider when we are in the midst of a great argument or drama that is playing out in our lives that the Elders view these things very much like when a mother sees her two-year-old scream, cry, and bop another child on the head with a stuffed animal. The mother doesn't want her child to fall apart, become hysterical and cry. She feels for her child, but at the same time, she sees a little bit of comedy in how seriously the child takes what is usually a trivial drama. She continues to love her child and thinks the world of it, hoping it will go on enjoying the day, living and learning.

This was a big light bulb moment for me, because I had entertained the dark idea, during my life, that every little less than perfect action of mine, was being "watched by God," and judged with anger or sadness. I felt constant guilt for my mistakes and belabored over the dread of "being watched" with severe or stern eyes. I felt that I was a disappointment to God. I wanted to please him, but I believed that I was so often falling short. I was frustrated and angry at my human faults. But here, no one was mad at me. I got the chance to view others from a much higher frequency which was wonderful. Also knowing how much Love I felt as I watched or sensed others in their personal situations, made me want to live more in the spirit of joy rather than guilt and worry.

I felt the higher part of me, which I call the SOUL, had compassion for the earthly ME that was so ignorant and juvenile. My soul seemed to understand in every detail what I was working with on earth. My soul wanted my earthly self to awaken, and be filled with Love and Joy. I wanted my earthly, child-like self to be kinder, to be more conscious, and to find Peace and balance.

I did not have an experience of seeing God as an "old man in a big white robe, sitting on a throne," although, that was the most prominent image I held in my mind from my earthly existence. From my NDE, God was the Mind, or maybe I'd say, "The Order" in all things. God was the Supreme Highest Vibration and Frequency. God felt like more of an ESSENCE than an old man, to me. God is ineffable; He was all around and in everything. Even using the name, "God" for what I experienced seems unfitting. God is so much more than what can be imagined through naming. And God no longer felt male to me. I didn't sense a gender, if there was one. The idea of gender seemed silly from the Other Side. God was all that is beautiful and peaceful and One, and all that is Good.

I'd also wondered at religion while I was there, and I quickly received the knowing that this wasn't important in the way I imagined it was prior to my NDE. I understood that one's religion, no matter which Church they joined or didn't join on earth, was what was written in their own heart. It was about WHO the person was, not what label they wore. It didn't matter on the other side who or what they worshipped or what religion they believed in. What matters is your own frequency, tone, and mathematical equation that represents YOU. You are who you are. I learned that we are here to learn how to divinely Love; to become masters of ourselves. We learn to rule our own lower or denser, aspects of self and to transmute these aspects upward to our highest possibility. We are all working toward Oneness again, as I concluded in part, from the experience.

While with my Guide, I was shown many planets and also some moons. I saw one planet or moon that appeared to be partially submerged in water! There are no words for how beautiful these scenes were. The colors were so vibrant and rich. I especially loved the hue of blues that I saw.

Were these colors what we see on earth? Yes and no. These colors exist, superimposed over what we see on earth. It is like there is a film or layers over the colors we see on earth, so we don't see them as vibrant and colorful as we do on the other side.

Finally, the planet Earth pulled up in front of me, or maybe we pulled up in front of it! It was magnificent!!! It was a floating marble, just swimming with color. I was ecstatic with awe.

I was able to move around the planet and feel different continents, countries, races, even certain smaller states, cities, and people! Each held its own kind of personal vibration and energetic pattern. This was fascinating to me! Each race, each country, even a state, each family in a way, is like its own organism. All are connected, but with an influence of its very own and very important unique purposes. Each is sacred and vital.

As I peered out over the planet, my Guide, told me to go back to where I came from. He wanted me to return to earth. He assured me that he would be there, waiting. At this, I turned to him and felt something I cannot put into mere words.

When I received his intention that I should return, it seemed as if he were my own perfect mother, who was going to turn and leave the toddler "me" in the middle of a foreign country. I felt like he was going to abandon me. It was so unexpected and seemed like something wrenched inside of me and instantly tore myself in half. I actually felt myself collapsing as I heaved and fell forward.

The emotional pain was so deep that I could hardly even cry out. It was as if the cry imploded within me and I felt like I was fracturing, leaving shards of glass all about a floor. I moaned while my emotional self poured out of me. It was like a cloud so heavy with rain it could no longer hold its moisture that was gushing downward like a waterfall. I wailed from a place inside of myself that I've never felt before. If there could be such a thing as spirit body existing with cells and organs, then they would all be bursting with anguish. Every part of me cried out. Telepathically, all I could express was, "NOOO!!!!!!"

I can't ever go through this part of my NDE without tears and a stinging pain in my chest. To leave him was the worst imaginable possibility.

It felt like death, separation, and division from my one and only. The devastation I felt was unbearable. Even when I remember parting from my Guide, it still feels like my heart is being scorched.

My Guide came closer to me while he calmly encouraged me to be strong. He told me to look to my left. As I did, I saw a school bus pull up in the distance. A small child was escorted out and brought to me. I recognized her as my own daughter, who at the time was only four years old. She had been asked in her sleep to come in spirit to help me. She walked up to me, tugged at me a little and sweetly said in an encouraging voice, "But Mommy? Who will take care of us?" Love on the other side is so much bigger, so much fuller than it is on earth. On the other side, I felt more honest with Love. When I was connected to the Source that was how I felt it and what I was connected to. I could not turn others away who are in need. There was no way I could have turned down my own daughter's plea. Without hesitation, I answered, "Oh honey, I will, of course!" My daughter was then escorted back to the bus.

My Guide smiled knowingly and reminded me that he was not forcing me to go back, despite what it felt like to me. I looked at him and back at the planet Earth, feeling so frightened. I still did not want to depart and separate from him. The pain of division still seared through me. I cried and told him that I wasn't sure I could do it.

He said, "Look to your right." I looked to my right and saw a holographic figure. It was my own mother. It was a view of her in the future, and she seemed tired and in need of help. I will not go into detail here, because I want to respect her privacy, but I felt myself lean toward this futuristic hologram with the desire to touch or help my mother somehow now, even though it wasn't presently occurring. The hologram felt alive to me. It seemed that as I leaned toward her, that I was a Gardener who wanted to prune some foliage.

The hologram faded out and my Guide said, "You see? It is time. YOU want to go." I knew I needed to, but still, I hesitated while anticipating my departure and loss of this One. I cried out, sobbing, "Please! I can't go without you!" There was a pause and then he answered, "Very well." All at once, I felt we were together. We were one. I was safe and calm. I heard him nudge me, "Point your finger forward. Touch the planet."

This might seem strange, but I reached and saw in form, my own finger reach forward and enter into the energetic field of the planet. I felt a surge of electricity run from the tip of my finger that began to move up. As the electricity hit the first knuckle, there was an unbelievable pulling sensation. Like a roller coaster ride that whipped me forward. Then I was back in my dark room at home still feeling disconnected from my body. My husband must have come to bed. He was there now, sleeping deeply. I could see both, him and myself. I moved toward my body and tried to connect and awaken it. I could not. I could not feel any sensation of my body at all. Then, I began to panic. I urgently pressed my husband to wake up, calling out to him, but my voice was not there. I continued trying to move my body from the inside and with no feeling of breath or life. I mentally screamed for help.

Then I felt my Guide there. I felt him say, "You must push yourself again and again through the throat area. This will trigger a release of energy and he will hear you. You must get him to touch you in order to connect with your body." I could not understand why this would work, but I began to rush through my throat area, over and over. Then I heard a noise come out of the mouth, as the mouth dropped open. It was like a creaking door, slowly opening or a low frog-like groan that was just air moving out.

My husband heard this, woke up, and asked, "Amy? What is it? What's the matter?" I couldn't answer. I tried to scream or cry out to him, but could not. He leaned over and I saw him shake me. I felt through his hands a level of electricity move through me. But I was unable to connect to my body or move. He got up and turned a light on. My eyes were still shut, but I witnessed the look on his face.

He suddenly went very pale and his mouth dropped open. Beads of sweat formed instantly around his hairline; he was perspiring heavily. I'd never seen such a frightened look on his face before. He grabbed me and yanked my body upward toward him, trying to hold me up, shouting, "AMY!! AMY, AMY!!!" Again and again, he yelled. He was trying to check my pulse. My head dropped back and he pulled my eyelids open. He was nearly screaming my name. As he continued to shake my body, I felt more and more electricity moving all around my body. Then, I felt something like a POP, and I was back in my body. I sucked in a long, deep breath and just hung there limply, breathing in and out. I took deep breaths.

After a few minutes, my husband was asking, "What should I do? Should I call 911?" I answered firmly, "No. I'm fine. Don't call anyone. I just need to sit down for a minute." I knew without a doubt that I was fine. He helped me to the other room where I sat on the couch. I tried to tell him what had happened. I didn't know where to begin.

It took me months to tell him all that I could remember. I still can't write it all here, because just the basics of all that I came to understand would take me weeks to write. I also continued to have visions, incredible dreams, and more experiences that included personal teachings and other very sacred happenings.

Here are some of the insights I learned from the other side. I understand now, that I have been through part of the integration process that usually takes 7 years for most NDErs to go through. I had the NDE when I was age 30 and shared it with NDERF at age 37. There are several things that have taken a while to find the words to explain the experience. Other things like emotions, I will never be able to fully describe because there is nothing like it on earth.

There are other things that I knew and have not been allowed to remember. I suspect that if I had remembered those things that it might have interfered with my lessons on earth. For instance, if I knew my Guide's name while with him, then it was taken from me upon return to my body. I wouldn't be shocked to discover that much memory was pulled from me in regard to personal details of my Guide, because even what memories I do have are painful for me and have made me crave to return to the other side. I do sense some parts of my NDE have been veiled to an extent.

I felt perfectly fine once I'd come back fully into my body. I refused any medical check-up. I was confident and at peace. My health has returned. I get stronger and stronger each year. The fibromyalgia did not instantly leave after my NDE. It was more of a process, such as eat the right healthy foods and by changing the way I thought into more positive, harmonious, and loving thoughts.

To my own surprise, I found the day after this event that I felt well enough, except that I could not eat any meat at all. Nor did I have any desire to. I've been a vegetarian since my NDE and I eat a lot of raw organic foods. I don't eat anything with chemical ingredients, and as advised during my NDE, for the most part I keep my food very pure. My children and husband eat mostly this way too. We are all feeling great.

On the other side, everything DID feel so good to me. I came back with this Knowing that despite what SEEMED "good" or "bad" on earth, now became united as only, "Good." I now trusted and knew that everything was in its rightful place. Even when people made decisions that I didn't agree with, I still felt that in the overall picture, it was ALL within the "Good." I had that Knowing that there was the essence or spark of the Highest or "God" in EVERYTHING. The Highest was in every atom, mineral, vegetable, animal, human, and beyond. I just Knew that the Highest waited within everything to expand, create, grow, and experience life. God is supreme Intelligence. And so much more.

I had never realized that my critical thinking and judgment of others was a source of all-encompassing misery for my soul. I call this my "duality" way of thinking because on earth there are always opposites in which to compare my earthly experiences to. For instance, I could judge someone on a scale of good, bad, or somewhere in between. If someone had walked up to me before my NDE and had asked me if my duality way of thinking was tiring and miserable for me, I would have been utterly confused and unable to agree with the statement or even make sense of it. I had never been aware of how my mind had always tried to label or judge everything in one way or another. Even good comparisons like "She's the nicest..." or "He's the best guy!" or "That backyard is the prettiest one, etc." was me judging one thing as better than another. Since coming back from my NDE, I find that in my earthly body and mind, this tendency still comes up occasionally, but not as often. I am much more conscious of when I am doing it. The duality of judging makes me feel physically sick. I don't feel such a need to do this now.

I lost all desire to analyze so much in life, as I'd learned before through religious examples and likely my own nature. I stopped trying to judge everything little thing for whether it was "good" or "bad." I wasn't so concerned with the label. I didn't want to frame anything into my perceptions. I now believe that we are all part of the Highest "consciousness" experiencing life. We learn how to love, create, and develop to the Highest we can be.

Looking back at that part of my experience, I was astounded by how earthly people can be on the Other Side. One might expect that upon entering through death's door, there would be sudden enlightenment. I know I expected that everyone would realize absolute goodness and choose the Light while looking for a fresh start. I expected people to become angelic and purified. But on the other side, everyone came in exactly as they'd been before. After my NDE, I now believe that some of the deceased, if not all, still have many earthly or worldly desires they had before they died.

I was able to explore the mind or energetic pattern of one of my earthly sworn enemies; someone I couldn't imagine forgiving for what I'd witnessed. Yet, coming back from my NDE, I could feel nothing less than a flood of Love for this woman. I wrote her a letter and told her how much I loved her. I asked for forgiveness for the energetic weight I might have held over her from my own dark thoughts and anger. I was writing as if she could have been my own firstborn; that is how much I adored her at that time. Because I was able to feel the Divine Love for her that the Essence of who God is, and how God feels toward her, I too, couldn't help but Love her in a similar way. The Higher Love of God moved through me. It was such a surprisingly marvelous feeling to relinquish the burden of my own anger and judgments, even that which I had subconsciously carried over the years. The release was so liberating!

In my earthly life, I have always had a mental block when it came to math. Even the simplest math ideas, starting from the time I was only six years old were difficult for me. I would mentally shut down when anything with numbers was presented to me. In my NDE, I was shown such an enormous array of gorgeous mathematical equations and visual numerical splendor. During that time, I was overjoyed at my own ability to thoroughly comprehend all of it. Unfortunately, upon my return, I was discouraged to find that I could not relay or bring with me the expansive amount of math understanding and knowledge I'd been so anxious to share with others. After the NDE, I am in love with numbers. That was at least a leap forward!

I found I was less materialistic since my NDE. Within the first week after my NDE, I was cleaning out my house and wanted to get rid of many things, a lot of decor, music CDs that I didn't find in harmony with the vibration I desired, etc. I lost my desire to want to shop as much as I had, previously.

I also had some paranormal "afterglow" experiences. I had a good couple of weeks after my return where I could see light in and around everything. I could also see into the realm that is around ours. I could see and feel the vibration of everything around me. All of my senses were much stronger. Too strong, even.

For instance, within a couple of days of coming back from my NDE, I stumbled upon a woman who was being consoled by many others. When everyone had dispersed, I asked her what was the matter, and she told me that she'd just found out that her daughter had died. She didn't know why or how she'd died. I asked to see a picture of her daughter, having the strong intuitive sense that I'd met her daughter on the Other Side.

The next day, she met me at my house. She had a black and white picture of her daughter, but I recognized her, right away. I said, "Did she have a pretty reddish color to her hair, and the most unusual green eyes?" She answered, "Yes, she did." I told her about my NDE; how her daughter spoke to me, and asked me to give information to her family. I told her all that I could remember her daughter telling me, and it all made perfect sense to the mother. She told me that shortly before her daughter's death she and her daughter had been estranged. Her daughter had begun to sing and had passionately loved singing. There was private information I was able to offer that gave this woman much comfort. I told her of her daughter's regrets in not having learned more while here on earth. We learned a week later or so, through the coroner, how she'd died. This confirmed for me, what the young woman on the Other Side had said to me about her drowning sensation and ultimately her death.

I did find that many of these paranormal experiences were interesting and enlightening. On the other hand, some of it was a little scary and disturbing. After some time, I willed this extra Sight to step back and let me get back to the basics, so to speak. And things did return to almost normal.

My spiritual practices are different. I am forever grateful for my Life Review and what I took from it. It is one of my favorite memories – and very different than what I believed it would be on earth. All of my earthly life, I had felt confusion and dismay at what I believed was lack of order. When I saw suffering that I deemed, unnecessary, sadness, or anything that I couldn't make sense of, I'd been riddled with a painful impression of Chaos. I was flabbergasted that the God I so fervently believed in, and was taught to trust, could do no better than what I beheld in my everyday life. It tore at my soul and I prayed daily and sometimes for hours and hours, begging for an answer that could provide some kind of a reckoning for my confusion.

I'd been taught that we had ONE life to live; I'd never even considered reincarnation. I couldn't understand why some people get to live in the most incredible luxury, and others are tested because God gave them terrible miseries to prove their strength. I had a hard time reconciling why people, like small innocent children all over the world, are born to suffer through starvation, disease, rape, mutilation, even years and years of torture, only to die and then get their just reward in heaven. This didn't seem like much of a "test" to me. It just seemed insane. I couldn't make logic of it. When I begged religious leaders for answers, I was told that "sometimes God let's wicked people torture good people so that He can punish the wicked for their deeds." The whole system just seemed sick to me. I couldn't completely respect this notion. But I wanted to believe that God had to be good.

Now, this Knowing from the NDE has helped me reconcile my earthly beliefs with what I experienced in my NDE. God, the Highest is pure love and goodness. I know to choose what feels right for me and to trust more than before. When something felt unjust or imbalanced, I Know to choose the action that would bring the most harmony, but to not worry about that which I had no control over. I know that eventually, even without our taking over the controls, the Universe is so full of order; it always finds a way to balance everything, because the Universe cannot exist without perfect balance. And the Highest and the Universe will continue to exist.

I could no longer continue with the religion I grew up in. This was not easy for me to walk away from, but I couldn't stay and maintain my own personal Truth and integrity. And yet, I have gratitude for having grown up in that religion and trust that it served its purpose for me. I am also at peace with the religious choices and needs of others.

I have continued to have the ability to reach, to a certain extent, my Guide. I began, right away to meditate, and connect with my Guide. My prayers became opportunities to connect, feel and receive rather than plead, worry and ask forgiveness. When I pray for others it is different. I am still while trying to connect to the Highest and then just calmly and peacefully try to offer a vision of the intended in Love and blessings, trusting in the Highest Will.

I still try to emulate Jesus, who has always been my example of how to live. But now I was less concerned with the technicalities of His story. I didn't care whether certain details were facts or not. I didn't care whether he was real or a myth. I knew it didn't matter because it was the principal of the teachings that mattered to me, now. I embraced the core teaching that was intended to be His Gift - "Do unto others as you would have them do unto you." From my NDE, I'd also understood other things about the original, uncorrupted "Christ Way." I've tried to hold to what I understand as concepts that held more original purity, which felt so much simpler to me.

I opened my reverence and respect to everyone who practiced the Golden Rule by doing good unto others. I found Good (God) in many places and within the teachings of many religions and ways of thought. Even within atheism, if a man believed in this principle, I could recognize the 'God' in him.

I have had many wondrous things happen in my life since the NDE. It would be too much to share here, but it's been the greatest thing that could ever happen to me. I still struggle with my own worldly and personal issues even though I feel more awakened and conscious.

I feel that every aspect of my NDE was a way for me to help me learn my earthly lessons. For instance: I had been pulled into that specific portal with others who had brought themselves to their own demise. This part of my NDE was to show me that for so many years I had been taking strong medications for my health problems that were slowly killing me. I had seen myself as a helpless victim for so long. In my pain and sorrows, I became totally self-absorbed and stagnant in all personal progress. I learned from seeing the others who had come through the portal, that I had to let go of myself and give up my personal story of being a victim. I gave up all the labels that doctors had given me for my health problems, and let go of the story of who I thought I was. I worked toward humility and try to open myself up to learning and growth. I took full responsibility for my own suffering and continue striving to blame no one or no thing. I continually try to bring back what I remember as the Perfect Love I experienced on the Other Side and become One with it.

Because of the very intimate relationship I have had with suffering, confusion and fear throughout my own life, my hope in finally allowing my near death experience to pay it forward. I share it with others for whatever possible service it might be to others who can relate on any level with pain; be it on the physical, emotional mental or spiritual plane.

I wouldn't want this kind of sharing held from me decades ago when I could have taken in some hope through something like this, so although with some admitted trepidation, I relinquish with love.
Amy.

Was the kind of experience difficult to express in words? Yes. The emotional aspect of the experience was so intense; I can't find words that are adequate.

At what time during the experience were you at your highest level of consciousness and alertness? While I was out amidst the stars with my Guide and I was being shown or downloaded with all kinds of Knowledge and Truth, I felt so absorbed and focused... so perfectly present in that moment, that I'd forgotten everything from my life on Earth. I forgot about my husband and children for the time being.

Did your vision differ in any way from your normal, everyday vision (in any aspect, such as clarity, field of vision, colors, brightness, depth perception degree of solidness/transparency of objects, etc.)? Yes. Everything was much more clear and vibrant. And you could view everything at many different levels. Not just surface.

Did your hearing differ in any way from your normal, everyday hearing (in any aspect, such as clarity, ability to recognize source of sound, pitch, loudness, etc.)? Yes. I heard things telepathically. So it doesn't compare. Everything was perfect because I didn't have to strain to hear anything.

Did you experience a separation of your consciousness from your body? Yes.

What emotions did you feel during the experience? I felt absolute elation, bliss, utter peace, and at times, sadness, despair and even fear. But each was relevant to what I was watching or learning or choosing to experience.

Did you pass into or through a tunnel or enclosure? Yes. But it was so fast, I guess that I don't recall this part well. I remember more of the sensation than what I saw. It was just a strong pull like a vacuum, and very fast from what I remember.

Did you see a light? Yes. I came into different areas, with different degrees of light. The Guide who was with me had so much Light coming from his face.

Did you meet or see any other beings? Yes. Those who were also moving through the portal. I saw many deceased beings.

Did you experience a review of past events in your life? Yes. All compassionate. My Guide stayed close by in support. I felt no judgment. I was only there to come to understand myself and others around me. It was wonderful and I felt relieved.

Did you observe or hear anything regarding people or events during your experience that could be verified later? Yes. I met a girl who had died. After my NDE, I had coincidentally found her mother and was able to verify that it was indeed her daughter who I'd met and been given personal information on. I suspect that the daughter had knowledge at the time that I would return to earth and meet her mother.

Did you see or visit any beautiful or otherwise distinctive locations, levels or dimensions? Yes. A lower, more astral-like place than earth; and a Higher, more beautiful and Light-filled place.

Did you have any sense of altered space or time? Yes. Time was different. I had a hard time placing the order of things when trying to explain in order what had happened to me. It felt like the experience had taken a very long time because I had been given so much information and knowledge. Yet, I don't think I could have been out of my body for too long and still survived. It may have only been minutes. I don't know for sure.

Did you have a sense of knowing special knowledge, universal order and/or purpose? Yes. I came to trust in all things. I realized there is Perfect Order in all. I also realized that God is the essence or breath of life that is in everything and everywhere. My understanding of what I need, religiously, became much simpler, basic and beautiful with two rules "Learn to Love" and "Cause no suffering."

Did you reach a boundary or limiting physical structure? Yes. I was very aware that one could not just take off and go absolutely anywhere. I sensed vibrational and frequency boundaries. If your own vibration held to a certain note, so to speak, or channel, it would be like hitting a brick wall to try and move through other places. The most refined could move through all vibrational frequencies.

Did you become aware of future events? In a way, yes I did. But I kept much of this to myself. I also knew that certain basic events could be stretched out or sped up due to our own choices as humanity. These things for me have been accurate, but I have no sense of time with these things. Everything I have perceived as "coming," feels like NOW, and yet, things happen here, chronologically, in an order and in time. It confuses me and I often choose to ignore what I sense.

Did you have any psychic, paranormal or other special gifts following the experience you did not have prior to the experience? Yes. For a while, I could see very well. I could even see at cellular level. I could see something as inanimate as a chair or curtain vibrating. This proved to be too much of a distraction after some time. I was so interested in the distractions that I couldn't focus on my daily routines. So, I asked to have it removed. I also can pull into a meditative like focus and receive answers to my own questions and visions and dreams that have been very prophetic for me and life-changing.

Have you shared this experience with others? Yes. At first, I only shared it with my husband. I came back quite confused. In the beginning, I was stunned and out of balance and was trying to describe things I couldn't yet describe, which made me feel like a fool. It took me a good year or two before I could logically explain in a way that sounded intelligible to others.

Did you have any knowledge of near death experience (NDE) prior to your experience? No.

How did you view the reality of your experience shortly (days to weeks) after it happened? Experience was definitely real. I knew without a doubt that it was real, but back in my own body and surrounded by the same things that I'd been immersed in before, I began to panic and question what my next step would be. I was afraid and wanted to go back to the Other Side. The world felt very frightening to me. I craved the peace that I'd felt on the Other Side. It took me some time to remember all that I'd learned, remind myself to always trust, and be at peace with where I currently was in my existence. It was a difficult transition.

TWO

The next NDE is a little atypical because of the life review. Most life reviews are where they person sees and feels their earthly life and then they judge themselves. However, Alexa's NDE has God, Jesus and the Devil in a courtroom setting. Generally, what we have found is that the NDE content is what helps the person grow spiritually. And that is what happened. Because of her NDE, she wanted to join a church that was very structured. The Latter Day Saints was the religion that came closest to her NDE. She feels that this is where she can grow the most spiritually.

ALEXA H.

I was 5 years old. After coming out of anesthesia from tonsillectomy, adenoidectomy, and tongue trimming, I was fully awake. I began to choking on ice cream. The doctor said, "There she goes again..." which always made me wonder if I had blacked out in Recovery... but I was in the Recovery room, so when did my heart stop? Anyway, I went to a velvet Blackness, with an all-knowing Intelligence, whose Love was unconditional. I didn't want to go back. I didn't understand WHY my mother and grandmother had allowed this stranger, the doctor, to hurt me so much. I loved being in the Blackness. I do know that as I started to pass out, they did chest compressions. Apparently, they did them the whole time I was out-probably minutes, because my chest hurt when I was aroused.

I remembered liking anesthesia; that was different from the Blackness; more like Sleep.

I did come back, against my Will. The doctor said, "Let's not let that happen again."

I never fully trusted my mother or grandmother afterwards.

I also could "Read" people, from that time on, so I credit the NDE as the start of my intuition abilities.

It was a long ride back to the house, and for once, my grandmother held me the whole way back to her house, where we lived. It was a cold, spring night in late March. I remember my grandmother holding me in a blanket. I didn't sleep - my throat hurt too much. My grandmother insisted on taking us home that night, but I do remember seeing the cold, white stars out the window.

On April 3, 1993, I had the MAJOR NDE. I had no brainwave or heartbeat for an extended amount of time and had an intense, detailed NDE:

I went into labor with my second child, after a long hot week. I was very tired from lack of sleep and the labor seemed "not quite right." Trying to relax was difficult, but we even had time to call our church from the hospital, and ask for prayer during the Wed night prayer meeting. Also, the childbirth class we had attended came by with a film crew. "Hey, we got some good footage!" they said. Like I could have cared! I just wanted to get this kid out! The baby's heartbeat slowed, and we went into the delivery room; I had just enough time for some anesthesia, and whammo! Out he popped. He was a "blue" baby, with the cord around his neck three times. He had been active in the womb, but now he was in trouble. He had fluid in his lungs and severe jaundice. They rushed him to Critical Care.

With the birth mirrors still in place, I looked up, and a ton of blood was still coming after the placenta delivered. "Is that MY blood?" I asked. It wouldn't stop flowing! I felt a tremendous weariness sweep over me. I tried to move my lips again, but even breathing was hard. I couldn't get out that I felt a cold, wrong-ness spreading over me!! "Doctor, I'm losing her..." I heard the nurse reading the numbers on the blood pressure meter as my pressure lowered; I saw the incredulous look in her eyes. I felt the Life force oozing out of me. I said a quick prayer inside myself:

"Oh Jesus, I hope you're everything I've been worshipping all these years! Please take care of my new little son; please take care of my beautiful daughter. I love them so much.

God I give You my Soul..."

And I was suddenly above my body! It seemed the most natural thing in the world! I had hands, feet, and everything was as normal; I was me in some sort of soft gown.

There I was, above my poor, limp body, and yet I felt fine. I was ME: body, personality, and NO TIREDNESS. I regarded the shell of my body. Gee! I don't look so bad! I thought. All my life I had been called "big boned', but I looked normal! I had always been compared to my 5 ft. tall, 100 lbs. sister! But here I was lying there—looking pretty and normal. I did notice that I didn't look like a mirror image. My body had more dimension. As I regarded this body, I was aware of all the emotion and frantic activity in the room. They were all so upset. "I can't find a pulse," said the nurse next to me. She was shocked. I had been a normal pregnancy. Another nurse said, "Where's the Crash cart?" I didn't know what a crash cart was, but it sounded important. They started CPR. I was sad they were so upset, but I was FINE. I had no, repeat no concern for my new baby or daughter; they were in God's hands. My husband, who had been rushed out of the room, looked totally bewildered, as hands pushed him through the doors. I knew he would be given Heavenly Guidance.

While all this was happening, a Light filled the room. The Doctor's arm was stuck in me far enough as to stuff a turkey; but the growing Light was increasing, and pure, soft, joyous. I saw it permeate every inch of the room. Even as I had lifted out of my body, there were Beings on both sides of me, as I observed all that. Forget cherubim, these were the BIG guys—HUGE, POWERFUL Angels, with even more powerful white feathered wings.

"Ooh, feathers," I remember thinking. I wanted to touch those wings so much; they looked so soft. There was one tiny feather within my reach...NO! As I reached, the Angels started to escort me; that was there job...and to keep me safe (from what? I wondered). We floated down or through a tunnel that had opened up from a small dark point. As we went towards the large, circular entrance, we left the room behind. We kept moving forward.

It was incredibly black and dark. The hospital room faded back into nothing. The Angels glowed softly, and I had no fear as we traveled to the speck of Light at the future end of our floating. There was a soft "whooshing," but I wasn't really listening. What I did notice was that the tunnel, itself, was as if it was made or had sectional parts (like a kids hoop in the back yard), which were joined by burning, yellow energy/flame-type rings, that didn't fully appear until AFTER we went through them! The "energy rings" were just were just like the rings or hoops in the Hopi walk, but I didn't know this till many years later.

As we passed through the rings and sections, a single tone would sound. I could see ahead and behind me, as we passed through the rings. They interested me at the time. The Angels on either side of me had NO interest in anything other than getting me to the enlarging Light. I felt totally at peace. The Angels never touched me; we were joined by some invisible power, like love. I was in no pain, from the hemorrhaging; I felt "whole."

Once we got to the end, the Angels disappeared or went off. I saw hundreds, maybe thousands of people all different sizes, shapes, and heights. Men and women (no children or wheelchairs) all dressed in a soft white, simple, plain long clothing, each with a gold sash at the waist. All were smiling and accepted me just as I was in my humanity. No one had a fault finding or critical attitude. The meeting was joyous, not scary. I did not see any family members, but I felt as if I was a member of a large, general family there.

Over to one side, on my right, was something amazing. I moved (floating not walking) over to look. There were steps, ivory, glowing steps. At the bottom of the steps were tiny spirit beings, cherubim? They were constantly singing the praises of God: HOLY HOLY HOLY TO THE LORD OF HOSTS; GLORY GLORY GLORY TO GOD; HOLY IS HIS RIGHTEOUSNESS, TRUTH AND POWER...They just went on and on. As they sang, I thought at first they each had three sets of arms, but they didn't; it was just one set each. The reason for thinking they had multiple arms was that all their arms were constantly moving at rapid speed. The arms covered their lips, ears, and eyes as they sang. I never fully understood the deep, symbolic meaning of those motions, but I know there was one. I now think it was: May what I say glorify the Lord God; May what I hear glorify the Lord God; May what I see glorify the Lord God, because that was each one's attitude. As well as arms constantly moving, each cherubim had wings that revved up and down slightly, beating all the time, with the intensity of worship. The wings made a slight buzzing sound, but it was soft, and there was no wind that came from the wings beating.

I would have been happy to stay there with them for all eternity. My Soul welled up within me to worship God with them; oh, how I wanted to kneel down and stay with them! The Light permeating everything was especially strong there. The steps led up to God, and such was His brightness, that I could not look directly at Him. It wasn't the crystal-like, prism-like Light, but rather because of His Holiness. Everything was beautiful! I was allowed/able to see Jesus, smiling at me. I was so overwhelmed, but happy, I could hardly react! Joyous is the word.

Suddenly, a podium appeared. Yes, the hundreds of beings were still watching me, angels, and God and Jesus in their glorious Firmament were now behind me. I had turned to my left and somehow moved slightly forward (although there was no real "direction"). I was in some sort of Courtroom. The crowds "over there" could see and hear everything that happened, and could share what I was feeling. They waited, as I did; no one spoke in the crowd, no one spoke to me.

Although Jesus apparently had moved and now stood slightly to my back left, I wasn't totally aware of Him at that time. Why? Because an Entity had appeared. After he appeared, my Life Review began. I was given to understand that that was what it was. This was awful.

EVERYTHING I ever thought, did, said, hated, helped, did not help, should have helped was shown in front of me, the crowd of hundreds and everyone like a movie. How mean I'd been to people, how I could have helped them, how mean I was (unintentionally also) to animals! Yes! Even the animals had had feelings. It was horrible. I fell on my face in shame. I saw how my acting, or not acting, rippled in effect towards other people and their lives. It wasn't until then, that I understood how each little decision or choice affects the World. The sense of letting my Savior down was too real. Strangely, even during this horror, I felt a compassion, an acceptance of my limitations by Jesus and the crowd of Others.

During this Review, the Evil being was there. I looked at him; he was handsome, not ugly. Black hair, medium build, dressed in a brown robe w/black cord at his waist, his eyes caught my attention. They were a black void! There was no life or goodness in them. Intense in every way, his only Purpose was to possess, own, control my very Soul and make me suffer!! I shrank back in horror. Every time, during the Review, that I erred or failed, he enjoyed it immensely. He would shout out, "THERE! See how she messed up?" He would accuse me, "Why didn't she do better? Or help more? She ought to be punished!" I was desolate. My few, little good works didn't and couldn't measure up to God's perfect standard. I deserved any punishment I got. My soul was desolate. I lay dreading what would happen.

Then, when it was over, a huge deep voice boomed out:

IS SHE COVERED BY THE BLOOD OF THE LAMB?
YES!

The courtroom disappeared, and the evil being, Satan, screamed! He hissed like a snake, turned and whirled like a tornado, but got smaller and smaller. He shrunk down to a pile of dust and pouf! Disappeared completely, after screaming in anger the whole time.

Everything in that setting was gone, except the Heavenly crowd and Jesus Christ. He gazed at me with INCREDIBLE love! He held out his nail pierced hands and wrists, that although healed completely, had the outline of the crucifixion marks. This was no wimpy Jesus. He was strong, powerful, tall as a ceiling, and shining all over! His long, white hair was nothing compared to his burning, liquid gold eyes. They burned with Purity, Joy, and Purpose. He opened his mouth, and I saw his tongue extend and heard a loud sound like a freight train! The rushing and roaring sound that came out was almost deafening. He spoke of who He was, and that he was my advocate with God the Father. I fell down in awe and worshipped Him with my very Soul. I cried with Joy like a baby. Just like the woman of old, I wanted to touch Him, but humbly just tried to touch the hem of his long, white simple gown. He stopped me point blank, as I gazed up at His glorious, loving smile. He loved and accepted me—totally. I was filled with peace and contentment.

A gigantic book appeared, with gold edges, and opened itself. It was as big as three buildings. A huge, lightening bold "finger" appeared. As it skimmed over the pages, they turned automatically. In this Book was the name of fathers, mothers, and their children. Also, the death dates if the person had died. The "finger" moved to my family's line.

THE DEEP VOICE AGAIN: IS IT HER TIME? NO!

In less than a blink, WHAM! I was back in my earthly body! OH YUCK! I was hot, sticky, sweaty, and h-e-a-v-y to the max! UGH. Forget about moving; it was hard to even breathe! I felt like a ton of bricks. I didn't like this at all!! Tears streamed down my cheeks. "I WANT TO GO BACK...BACK," I croaked out.

The nurse looked down at me with a radiant face, "Welcome home," she said. "We lost you there for a while." Then she realized what I said. "Back? Where would you go? Don't you want to see your baby?" Remembering my glorious experience, I blurted out, "No! My baby's fine; he's in God's hands I'm sure. I want to go BACK! Please let me go back."

"Oh!" she said, "Were you in that place where it's all white, and you saw Jesus?" Yes, I replied. "Is it as beautiful as they say?" she asked. Yes.

She leaned toward me and said, "We've had this happen BEFORE! I hope I get to go there." I sighed in resignation.

The doctor and his staff looked like they'd been through the wringer. My mouth finally worked better, and I apologized for "keeping" them so long. They just looked at each other numbly. The next morning, the doctor came to visit me on "Rounds." He said he'd gotten 3-4 hours of sleep and held my hand for a moment. I was shocked. Back then, doctors hardly gave you the time of day. He said softly, "When you're ready, I'd like you to tell me what happened. I lost you one, two times really, on the table. Can you tell me now?" What? I thought. OH THAT...and I grabbed my head and moaned, as the memory came flooding back. It felt like my head was exploding for a few minutes. "Are you in pain?" "No," I replied, "it just all came flooding back. I actually feel GREAT!" and I did. After I got used to remembering it all in record speed, I adjusted, and felt better than ever! I smiled up at him. He left, after getting me to promise to tell him later.

Weeks later I did call the doctor; he put his other calls on Hold. He listened and told me that he had seven women from my Church, that had almost identical experiences; six women from other churches. He was so kind and encouraging.

After that and when I was healed, I went to a Wed night prayer meeting.

Those women could really pray fervently! When we were done, they paused and looked at me. "You know, Alexa, you look different; did anything happen after your son's birth?" I smiled and said I'd had an Experience. They smiled and understood! It was THEM- we'd all found each other! It was glorious.

After my NDE I knew I was to raise my children to be Christians, strong ones. In my family filled with divorce that would be an accomplishment! My paternal great grandmother had lost her second child, a boy; I always felt my second child, my son with my Near Death Experience, was the offset to that loss.

I gave him to God; he is now a Minister serving God. Both he and my daughter love the Lord. I am Blessed.

THREE

William is dear friend of mine. His NDE is a good example of why we have the questions. Even though the initial narrative is rather brief, there are juicy details under many of the questions. The questionnaire serves as a way to hone in and expand on many details that might be less detailed when the experiencer is writing the experience in the narrative format. William has had several NDEs, but the deepest NDE has a lot of spiritual wisdom to share with others.

William talks about us being eternal beings. He details how we have a group of souls who we travel together with to learn lessons. He calls them the guardians.

William's NDE is what I call an "integrative" sharing because he submitted the questionnaire at two or more times over the course of several years. Many times a person will fill out the form shortly after they have the NDE. At that time, many people will be confused. Some will be angry at coming back and many will be baffled at how they could be dead and still have this amazing experience. Later on, they will fill out the form after processing the NDE and integrating into their waking reality. This usually results in a more thorough narrative because they now have words and can explain more about their experience. They may also be more loving and compassionate with the new changes they've integrated into their lives. Here, William was fairly rebellious against organized religion, he was coming to terms with his enhanced intuition, and he was trying to make sense out of what he learned on the other side. Since the time of the first questionnaire,

William made the decision to go back to school so he could teach others. He changed his life from working in a casino, to service to others. He also learned how to integrate his NDE with his religion for a deeper and more loving understanding of the gospels. His experience was powerful enough for him to change, but it also was spiritually transformative for others.

WILLIAM SI.

The first part of my experience, the part of leaving my body, is much the same as in all the NDE books and lectures that I have attended and read. However, during the course of my NDE, what I "felt" and "understood" was in was quite extraordinary. This happened during the passage through the tunnel, which was like a shaft of light. Passing through this area, seemed as if it could be endless, yet wasn't. I could sense those spirits that were in the shadows; and I understood why they wouldn't look into the light. These spirits felt they were not worthy to look into the light because of actions they had done in the human existence. These poor souls were afraid or bound by their earthly beliefs from religious indoctrination. Therefore, they stayed in the shadows rather than going to the light.

I came to the end of the tunnel and saw the most beautiful garden ever (I had been here two times before as this was my third NDE).

All that I experienced on that side, all that I remember, I could not include here, it would take too much typing to put it all in. What I can say is that the experience profoundly changed my life. It changed my perceptions about what life is all about. My story has also affected many other people just by sharing my story with them.

I'm not afraid of death or dying. I don't even care how I die. I have a promise made to me by my Heavenly Father, the moment my mission in this existence is over, I will leave immediately and I don't care how I go out. I just want to go home.

Was the kind of experience difficult to express in words? Yes, it is very difficult to express, as there is nothing on earth that can compare to the beauty and wonder of the realm beyond this one.

At the time of this experience, was there an associated life-threatening event? The first NDE was due to an allergic reaction to the anesthesia during the surgery, and in combination with a heart murmur. The second and the third were associated with a life threatening condition. The second was caused by cardiac arrest and I was clinically dead for 15 minutes. The third was from a ruptured appendix, and two days after surgery my body temperature was last recorded at 85 degrees and my organs were beginning to shut down in preparation for my body to die.

At what time during the experience were you at your highest level of consciousness and alertness? Physically, minimally alert. Spiritually and consciously, extremely alert. To the point that I vividly recall all that I saw and the conversations that I had with those on the other side.

I would have to say this occurred about halfway through my last NDE. My last NDE was not one single trip but actually seven trips. I would leave my body, not only to escape the tremendous pain I was in, but also to continue those things that I was being instructed in on the other side. It was during the third or fourth trip when I was taken into a room that had a large wheel on the floor. At the end of each spoke of the wheel stood a pillar. The wheel had 12 spokes and subsequently there were 12 pillars at the end of each spoke. Each pillar also contained 12 crystals and 12 symbols. Of the symbols on each of the pillars, they were not read as a column, but each symbol created a type of ring with all the other pillars. The first symbol on one pillar related to the first on the next and so on. Some of these symbols were representative of the astrological star constellations of the zodiac. Others pertained to symbols that I would become familiar with as time progressed and I would know them when they appeared. During this time, I was surrounding by those I call the ancient ones. The ancient ones each stood on a spoke and placed their left hand on a pillar and their right hand upon my head. I have been asked several times who the "ancient ones" are or were. I can testify to you, the ancient ones are not so much in accordance to their earthly age, but to their eternal celestial age.

The ancient ones, are men and women who have been chosen, from the beginning and before the creation of this world. They were chosen for the counsel of Heaven to be servants of our Heavenly Father and our Lord Jesus Christ, and during this lifetime, they chose to be upon this earth. The ancient ones are the prophets, teachers, apostles and leaders of old and the not so distant past.

Well, I can and I can't say what the symbols were. Some of them I know what they were and why they are there; others, I know them when I see them and also know how to use them.

First: 1 set of the symbols were those of the zodiac, but not as we know them, but their astrological star constellations. Whether some want to believe it, those symbols do have a correlation to events or occurrences that have or will happen on this earth or in an individual's life. It is really more complex than even some astrologers have ever delved into.

Second: Another set of the symbols pertain to the healing art of Reiki as we call it here. I know all of the symbols, and how to use them, as I'm also a Reiki Master. I hate to burst anyone's bubble, but some of these "new" symbols that Reiki Organizations have come out with are nothing but marks, they do nothing.

Third: Another set, pertains to wisdom, knowledge and understanding. This one is extremely difficult to explain as it more involves senses and feelings. They are keys that help in unlocking "mysteries" that we have often thought we would never know. They also help in enhancing psychic abilities.

Besides the symbols, there were also crystals that go with each symbol. Of course, the most powerful of all crystals is a diamond. A clear or semi-clear quartz ball can be used for all the symbols as it resonates all colors. Yet besides the crystals, those crystals also held colors and they too are important to our psyche and to our overall health and well being.

To tell people what these symbols are, it isn't easy to explain something there is no reference to. Many of them I can't explain, because I just use them every day, they are like second nature to me. Just as my psychic abilities I've always had, even now this gift is more pronounced.

How did your highest level of consciousness and alertness during the experience compare to your normal every day consciousness and alertness? It was during this time of me standing in the center of the circle (wheel) that my consciousness and alertness were at their highest. I was aware of what each one of the ancient ones spoke to me about and what they were blessing me with. As there were no physical words spoken, their words were communicated by pure thought. There could be no misunderstanding of any part of their communication. How this differs from my normal consciousness and alertness is quite different as I have a hearing problem and sometimes being able to fully concentrate on what people are saying can be very difficult.

Was the experience dream like in any way? No, it was real. The only thing I have to add to this is, while I was in my experience, I had the pleasure of having a discussion with Jesus. I knew it was him and that I can never deny. I also received a wonderful hug from him. I felt his body with my spirit. There are times, especially when I do have occasional bouts of depression, I can still feel his physical body with my fingertips. I know he was real and what he brought to the world was wonderful.

Did your vision differ in any way from your normal, everyday vision (in any aspect, such as clarity, field of vision, colors, brightness, depth perception degree of solidness/transparency of objects, etc.)? Extremely, as in my physical form, I am extremely near-sighted and have to wear glasses. In my NDE, to be able to see clearly and be able to take in everything around me with the utmost clarity is one thing that completely amazed me. The colors on the other side are of the brightest colors, which our most florescent colors on this earth are muddy to the brightness and vividness of the colors that are in Heaven.

Did your hearing differ in any way from your normal, everyday hearing (in any aspect, such as clarity, ability to recognize source of sound, pitch, loudness, etc.)? Yes.

In my physical body, I am deaf in one ear and diminished in the other, yet during my experience the perception of sound was extremely acute. I could hear not only the birds singing, but everything in Heaven resounds with love of our Heavenly Father. No music on this earth comes close, yet I still listen for it.

Did you experience a separation of your consciousness from your body? That I could definitely say is a resounding yes. While in my physical body, I not only could feel the pain that I was in from the surgery, I could also feel the weak feeling from all the poison from the infection that was raging through my body. While I was on the other side, I had no feeling of pain, worry or any other ache of pain. My body felt whole and in a perfected state.

I could see myself as I am now, yet in a perfected state. I was a bit overweight in my physical form, yet I was in perfect form on that side. My hair was past my shoulders, yet was white, like spun glass.

In my physical form, I was also a bit overweight. Yet on the other side, I could see myself in my perfect form. What is amazing is that this memory of myself in my perfect form has not been removed or blocked from my memory. In my perfect form, I was about 35 years old, my present height of 6'-0", and my weight was around 175. There was only the minimum amount of fat on my body. I no long had my receding hairline, yet my hair was wavy, like it is when I grow it out in my physical form. Yet my hair was just past my shoulders and pure white. My eyes were still the clear blue that I have in this earthly existence.

What emotions did you feel during the experience? Humility, joy, happiness, sadness when I had to leave.

Did you pass into or through a tunnel or enclosure? Yes, my guardians led me into the tunnel. They were three men who were dressed in radiant white. These three men were also three of my best friends who had been with me throughout eternity.

Did you see a light? Yes. I saw a light that had a brightness greater than the noonday sun, yet it did not burn.

Did you meet or see any other beings? Yes, as I just mentioned my guardian angels guided me to the tunnel of light. We choose our guardian angels prior to coming to earth. I also came to realize that one of the things that we know, from the pre-existence, is that we will have our guardian angels that will work with the Holy Ghost to lead and guide us. We don't always listen, but they are there still the same. As I mentioned that we choose them, and they choose us. It is like a celestial contract bound with love.

The reason I'm saying this is very simple. We are all each other's guardians. Each one of our guardians has already come to this existence. At the time they were on the earth, we were each other's guardian angels. There are four of us in the soul family. Of me and my guardians, I know that they have preceded me to this earth and that I am the last of the four to come to earth. All three of their missions have been served on this earth; I'm in the process of serving mine. I also know that I was shown my mission on earth. I was not allowed to remember it though. However, I was allowed to set forth event markers along my path to know that I am following my path as it should be.

When we choose our "three guardian angels", they are not the only ones we choose. We also choose a total of 12 beings, yourself being one of the 12. Each of these other guardians are there for many other aspects of your life, yet a person will always have the 3 main guardians. Each person, including you, has served in this same capacity at some point in course of the eternities.

Did you experience a review of past events in your life? Yes. As time has passed, I look back over my life review in a more different light than I had originally. I don't look at it as a vision backward, but instead of seeing how I have followed my path. I saw that I didn't quite follow it at times, but that I was never far from it at any time. I also saw how I could have handled situations better at the time and how I can handle similar situations in the future.

Did you have any sense of altered space or time? Yes. There is no time on that side.

Did you see or visit any beautiful or otherwise distinctive locations, levels or dimensions? Yes. I have already written about the room with the wheel, but there was more. I was given a review of our world and our existence, from the beginning. I was there at the council in Heaven when the plan of Salvation was discussed and accepted. We all were there. This existence on earth was created in the spirit before it was created in the physical form. How awesome it is to not only look down upon this earth and see the aura of it as it radiates out. To know the Earth's aura is made up, not only from the planet itself, but from each and every living soul on this earth. The Earth's aura is the most brilliant blue. Even our sky does not compare to the radiance of this aura.

Did you have a sense of knowing special knowledge, universal order and/or purpose? Yes. I already had a basic understanding of what Heavenly Father had planned out for all of us on this world and especially on how the world was created. I didn't fully understand it until my last NDE. Even now, there is a part of my understanding that is there, but it is blocked because the understanding of the fullness of what it really means is not ready to come forth.

I came to understand that life, as we know it now is also an illusion. Since my NDE, I acquired a beautiful crystal ball. For one thing, as I gaze into it, I can see our existence as I saw it on the other side. There is no time, which is our measurement. What we need to experience, we can do so at whichever "time" would best suit that experience for us to gain that understanding.

Did you reach a boundary or limiting physical structure? No.

Were you involved in or aware of a decision to return to the body? Yes.

I was given a choice about my returning. I was also told that the things I had put into motion during my life would continue to their completion, but I wouldn't be there to enjoy them as I'm supposed to, if I chose to stay. I understood that I needed to return. I was sad, but I also knew that my return would actually be quicker than snapping my fingers when it was time.

What emotions did you experience following your experience? Anger, frustration, depression, crying spells, thinking I had made a big mistake coming back.

Did you become aware of future events? Not in the respect of wars, earthquakes, etc. Just a more heightened awareness of what will happen on a personal level.

Did you have any psychic, paranormal or other special gifts following the experience you did not have prior to the experience? Yes. I was born psychic, although I prefer the term "intuitive." However, my NDEs have magnified my abilities. I do not believe in predicting someone's future, yet I do know that as we pass through this existence that we do leave an energy imprint upon people, places and things. I use my abilities to help others and never for personal gain. I have helped the police in solving crimes and have helped people to bring closure to emotional pain in their lives.

Have you shared this experience with others? Yes.

Did you have any knowledge of near death experience (NDE) prior to your experience? No.

How did you view the reality of your experience shortly (days to weeks) after it happened? Experience was definitely real.

How do you currently view the reality of your experience? Experience was definitely real.

Has your life changed specifically as a result of your experience? I would say that my life has changed since I first filled out this questionnaire.

Have your relationships changed specifically as a result of your experience? Yes. It changed for a while with my wife and children, but they soon could see how it changed me in helping them. Relationships with my extended family members, well, not so good. They always thought I was crazy, and now they think I've really gone off the deep end. They are a closed-minded lot, and are not very receptive to change.

Have your religious beliefs/practices changed specifically as a result of your experience? Yes, I was active in the church. For a time after my last NDE, I left the church to pursue, search and understand what had happened to me. I had known that my intuitive abilities had dramatically increased; yet I still felt empty and angry for having to return. I returned to my faith, because I found that what I was really seeking was within my own beliefs all along. Now, I will say that from my NDE I have a deeper understanding about many beliefs. My spiritual depth and understanding of the Gospel is much stronger. My faith and trust in God and Jesus cannot be changed or altered. I know that Heavenly Father is not the angry, vengeful God that I was raised to believe as a child. He is a loving, caring, compassionate father that truly does care about his children.

Following the experience, have you had any other events in your life, medications or substances, which reproduced any part of the experience? No.

Did the questions asked and information you provided so far accurately and comprehensively describe your experience? Yes.

Any associated medications or substances with the potential to affect the experience: No.

FOUR

Anita Moorjani has been part of NDERF since 2006. She initially shared her experience with us and then was very active on the bulletin board. Her spiritual insight and willingness to share her experience has been remarkable and touched a lot of lives. Since this time, she has shared the entire story and her insights in a New York Times best-selling book, "Dying to be me" published by Hay House. She chronicles her life, with details of her journey through cancer, the NDE, and subsequent healing.

Anita was raised Hindu, but now is Buddhist, and is from Hong Kong. Her NDE is a prime example of a Non-Western NDE. The importance of sharing a Non-Western NDE shows that culture, ethnic and religious upbringing doesn't affect the content of the NDE. This means that NDE is a human experience and not confined to upbringing or prior beliefs. She had Hodgkin's Lymphoma. Interestingly, she had choice whether to return to her body or not. Her decision to return actually affected the results of her blood tests taken prior to the NDE.

ANITA M.

I had cancer (Hodgkin's Lymphoma), and on this morning, I could not move. My husband rushed me to hospital, where, after doing scans, they diagnosed me with grade 4B lymphoma (the highest grade). The senior oncologist looked at my report and told my husband that it was too late, and that my organs were now shutting down. I only had 36 hours to live. However, the oncologist said he would do whatever he could but prepared my husband that I would most likely not make it, as my organs were no longer functioning. They started me on a chemotherapy drip as well as oxygen, and then they started to take tests, particularly on my organ functions, so that they could determine what drugs to use.

I was drifting in and out of consciousness during this time, and I could feel my spirit actually leaving my body. I saw and heard the conversations between my husband and the doctors taking place outside my room, about 40 feet away down a hallway. I was later able to verify this conversation to my shocked husband. Then I actually "crossed over" to another dimension, where I was engulfed in a total feeling of love. I also experienced extreme clarity of why I had the cancer, why I had come into this life in the first place, what role everyone in my family played in my life in the grand scheme of things, and generally how life works. The clarity and understanding I obtained in this state is almost indescribable. Words seem to limit the experience – I was at a place where I understood how much more there is than what we are able to conceive in our 3-dimensional world. I realized what a gift life was, and that I was surrounded by loving spiritual beings, who were always around me even when I did not know it.

The amount of love I felt was overwhelming, and from this perspective, I knew how powerful I am, and saw the amazing possibilities we as humans are capable of achieving during a physical life. I found out that my purpose now would be to live "heaven on earth" using this new understanding, and also to share this knowledge with other people. However I had the choice of whether to come back into life, or go towards death. I was made to understand that it was not my time, but I always had the choice, and if I chose death, I would not be experiencing a lot of the gifts that the rest of my life still held in store. One of the things I wanted to know was that if I chose life, would I have to come back to this sick body, because my body was very, very sick and the organs had stopped functioning. I was then made to understand that if I chose life, my body would heal very quickly. I would see a difference in not months or weeks, but days!

I was shown how illnesses start on an energetic level before they become physical. If I chose to go into life, the cancer would be gone from my energy, and my physical body would catch up very quickly. I then understood that when people have medical treatments for illnesses, it rids the illness only from their body but not from their energy so the illness returns. I realized if I went back, it would be with a very healthy energy. Then the physical body would catch up to the energetic conditions very quickly and permanently. I was given the understanding that this applies to anything, not only illnesses—physical conditions, psychological conditions, etc. I was "shown" that everything going on in our lives was dependent on this energy around us, created by us. Nothing was solid - we created our surroundings, our conditions, etc. depending where this "energy" was at. The clarity I received around how we get what we do was phenomenal! It's all about where we are energetically. I was made to feel that I was going to see "proof" of this first hand if I returned back to my body.

I know I was drifting in and out between the two worlds, but every time I drifted into the "other side", I was shown more and more scenes. There was one which showed how my life had touched all the people in it - it was sort of like a tapestry and showed how I affected everyone's lives around me. There was another which showed my brother on a plane, having heard the news I was dying, coming to see me (this was verified to me as when I started to come round, my brother was there, having just got off a plane). I then saw a glimpse of my brother and me and somehow seemed to understand it was a previous life, where I was much older than him and was like a mother to him (in this life, he is older than me). I saw in that life I was very protective towards him. I suddenly became aware he was on the plane to come and see me, and felt "I can't do this to him - can't let him come and see me dead". Then I also saw how my husband's purpose was linked to mine, and how we had decided to come and experience this life together. If I went, he would probably follow soon after.

I was made to understand that, as tests had been taken for my organ functions (and the results were not out yet), that if I chose life, the results would show that my organs were functioning normally. If I chose death, the results would show organ failure as the cause of death, due to cancer. I was able to change the outcome of the tests by my choice!

I made my choice, and as I started to wake up (in a very confused state, as I could not at that time tell which side of the veil I was on), the doctors came rushing into the room with big smiles on their faces saying to my family "Good news – we got the results and her organs are functioning – we can't believe it! Her body really did seem like it had shut down!"

After that, I began to recover rapidly. The doctors had been waiting for me to become stable before doing a lymph node biopsy to track the type of cancer cells, and they could not even find a lymph node big enough to suggest cancer (upon entering the hospital my body was filled with swollen lymph nodes). They did a bone marrow biopsy, again to find the cancer activity so they could adjust the chemotherapy according to the disease, and there wasn't any in the bone marrow. The doctors were very confused, but put it down to me suddenly responding to the chemo. Because they themselves were unable to understand what was going on, they made me undergo test after test, all of which I passed with flying colors, and clearing every test empowered me even more! I had a full body scan, and because they could not find anything, they made the radiologist repeat it again!

Because of my experience, I am now sharing with everyone I know that miracles are possible in your life every day. After what I have seen, I realize that absolutely anything is possible, and that we did not come here to suffer. Life is supposed to be great, and we are very, very loved. The way I look at life has changed dramatically, and I am so glad to have been given a second chance to experience "heaven on earth".

Was the kind of experience difficult to express in words? Yes. The experience was much more than words can express. Putting words to it makes the experience smaller and more limited. What I saw, perceived, and felt, and the clarity I experienced about life, was more than anything we are able to conceive, so words have not been created to describe it.

At the time of this experience, was there an associated life-threatening event? Uncertain. I was dying of cancer, and the doctors had said I only had about 36 hours to live. It was at this point where I started drifting between another dimension and this one.

At what time during the experience were you at your highest level of consciousness and alertness? Probably at the time when I was given the choice whether to go back.

How did your highest level of consciousness and alertness during the experience compare to your normal every day consciousness and alertness? More consciousness and alertness than normal.

If your highest level of consciousness and alertness during the experience was different from your normal every day consciousness

and alertness, please explain: I was going in and out of consciousness, so I was aware of both "sides". I was also aware of conversations taking place outside the room, beyond my earshot.

Did your vision differ in any way from your normal, everyday vision (in any aspect, such as clarity, field of vision, colors, brightness, depth perception degree of solidness/transparency of objects, etc.)? Yes. I was aware that I was still in the room - even though to others, my eyes were closed and I was not awake, I was still able to "see" everyone in the room, and at the same time experience the other dimension, as if it existed simultaneously.

Did your hearing differ in any way from your normal, everyday hearing (in any aspect, such as clarity, ability to recognize source of sound, pitch, loudness, etc.)? Yes. I was able to hear what was being said by the doctors and my family outside the room, well out of earshot.

Did you experience a separation of your consciousness from your body? Uncertain.

What emotions did you feel during the experience? Felt tremendous love, more than anything I have experienced on earth. I felt very loved, like no matter what I did, I would still be loved. I did not have to do anything to deserve it or prove myself.

Did you pass into or through a tunnel or enclosure? No.

Did you see a light? No.

Did you meet or see any other beings? Yes. I was surrounded by many beings, including my father and my best friend who had passed on. I did not recognize the other beings, but I knew they loved me very much and were protecting me. I became aware that they were there all the time, even when I was not aware of it.

Did you experience a review of past events in your life? No.

Did you observe or hear anything regarding people or events during your experience that could be verified later? Yes. I saw and heard a conversation taking place between my doctor and my husband outside of my room and down a hallway. I saw my brother on a plane coming to see me. Both of these were verified, including the conversation between my doctor and husband, which I repeated word for word.

Did you see or visit any beautiful or otherwise distinctive locations, levels or dimensions? No.

Did you have any sense of altered space or time? Yes. I felt I was in the other dimension a lot longer than I really was. The amount I saw and learned would have taken a lot longer in this dimension. Also, with the medical tests that were done, even though the tests were done, the results were dependent on my choice of whether to come back into life or not. That really changed my concept of time!!

Did you have a sense of knowing special knowledge, universal order and/or purpose? Yes. The clarity was amazing! I understood why I had the cancer, I understood how people get what they do, and I understood that life is a gift, but we don't realize it. I understood that we are very, very loved, no matter what. We don't have to do anything to prove ourselves to god, and there is no "heaven" or "hell". I realized we create our own heaven or hell here on earth, and I learned the key ingredients for creating my own heaven on earth!

Did you reach a boundary or limiting physical structure? Yes. I reached the point where I felt I had to make the choice whether to go back to life or onward into death. My best friend was there (who had died of cancer 2 years before) and she told me that this was as far as I could go or I would not be able to turn back. "You have come to the edge. This is as far as you can go" she said. "Now go back and live your life fully and fearlessly".

Did you become aware of future events? Yes. I was aware my body would heal very quickly, and it did. I was aware that all the tests would show phenomenal results, and they did. They found no trace of any disease on my scans, my biopsies, etc. My organs are functioning normally, my appetite came back, and I was made aware all of this would happen. It has only been 6 months since my NDE, and I am still awaiting all the other gifts that were shown to me. However, I can see my life changing in a direction where all of this is very possible. One of the things I saw was a very long life ahead of me!

Did you have any psychic, paranormal or other special gifts following the experience you did not have prior to the experience? Yes. I have been much more intuitive since the experience. When I am alone, I often get the awareness of being surrounded by beings (the same beings I felt when I crossed over), and being very, very loved - that same feeling I got during the NDE.

Have you shared this experience with others? Yes. Within days after it happened, as soon as I was well enough to talk, I started sharing it with my close family members - my husband, my brother (who I had seen on the plane), my mother. We were all very emotional and in tears. And they were all shocked with my account of events, the test results which I knew would be normal because I chose to come back, the conversations I "heard". Then they saw the speed of my recovery, the shock of the doctors who could no longer find any trace of cancer - it has changed my whole family. I also shared with my best friend who has been by me during this experience, and it has changed her life too. Going out and meeting people after coming out of hospital changed a lot of people, because the last they saw or heard of me, I was on my death bed! I had looked very, very sick, and could not walk or breathe properly at that time. Now I looked totally healthy and normal. The first time I walked into a group gathering after coming out of hospital, everyone's jaw dropped. They looked at me as if they had seen a ghost. They could not believe how quickly I had recovered - everyone thought I was going to die! Then I shared my experience with everyone in the room, and all of them believed me because they had seen the "before" and "after". Some of them said I had changed their lives.

Did you have any knowledge of near death experience (NDE) prior to your experience? Yes. I have read about NDEs but never expected to experience one. My NDE felt completely different to anything I have read because there was no light, tunnel, no religious figure, and I did not see my whole life flash before my eyes. While I was experiencing it, I had no idea that I was experiencing an NDE or an out of body experience. It felt very normal at the time. It was only after that I realized I had slipped to another dimension.

How did you view the reality of your experience shortly (days to weeks) after it happened? Experience was definitely real. I knew it was real because nothing else could explain the miraculous way my cancer just disappeared from my body! (I have the scans and medical tests to prove it)! And the charge I felt from the empowerment and the understanding - nothing else could explain the shift I felt in my way of thinking!

Were there one or several parts of the experience especially meaningful or significant to you? The whole thing was very powerful - I cannot imagine anything more empowering happening to me. However, two main things impacted me - one was being able to change the outcome of the test results. That made me realize that nothing is solid (or real). We can change anything. The second thing, even more impacting, is how my body went from being almost dead from cancer to totally healthy without a trace of illness in such a short time! It not only makes me feel that everything (including cancer) is not real (a shift in consciousness made it disappear!) but it also makes me feel very powerful, and I have a totally different understanding of life now.

How do you currently view the reality of your experience? Experience was definitely real. First of all, I am enjoying the wonders of my healthy body. I haven't felt this way in a while!

Secondly, I feel very "connected" in a way I never have before. Sort of "guided". I don't feel afraid of anything anymore. I know I won't die until I complete everything I came here to do. And even then, I am not afraid of death. Many, many more "coincidences" have been occurring in my life since the experience (hence the "guided" feeling). Things have been falling into my lap when I have wanted them, the right people call, I have been bumping into the right people, getting e-mails which answer questions I need answered, etc. Life has just become a lot easier, however it has only been a few months since I have been well. I am still feeling very high, and at the moment am still feeling the reality of the whole thing.

Have your relationships changed specifically as a result of your experience? Yes. I have become even closer to my family, but my social circle has changed. A lot of my friends have drifted away from me, but a small handful have got closer to me than ever, and I have made a lot of new friends since this experience.

Have your religious beliefs/practices changed specifically as a result of your experience? Uncertain. I was never very religious to begin with. I still don't believe in any particular religion, however this has strengthened my belief in spirituality, and my faith in the afterlife, and the power of our own higher self (soul).

Following the experience, have you had any other events in your life, medications or substances which reproduced any part of the experience? Yes. I am able to go back to that "connected" feeling of being loved, and feeling the other beings surrounding me, particularly when I am sitting still in a quiet environment.

Did the questions asked and information you provided so far accurately and comprehensively describe your experience? Yes.

FIVE

Birthe submitted her experience in Danish. Then it was translated by a volunteer and put on the website in Danish and in English. The tendency for wordiness and awkward phrasing is primarily due to the fact that words don't translate exactly from one language to the next. However, this does show that NDEs are similar across different cultures. There are many remarkable events in Birthe's experience, including the OBE and hovering by the ceiling, meeting deceased relatives, and meeting beings she knew prior to earth. She even met her soul cluster group. These are souls who travel through time with us.

The most remarkable part of this experience is the life review. Even though she had a guide who reviewed her life with her, it was used as a learning tool on how to do good on earth. She has a detailed description of all she learned from her life review and what she needed to know to be successful after she came back. Although it is typical for a person to return to earth for the sake of their children, this is the first time that the spiritual voice of the newborn convinced her to come back to her body. The infant had a foot in both worlds, heaven and earth.

BIRTHE L.

It was the 11th of February 1996. I had postpartum preeclampsia after the birthing of my youngest son the day before. My son, who is my tenth child, fortunately was healthy and doing fine after the birth. He is now 17 and still extremely healthy.

I gave a normal birth to my son, which lasted 1 hour and 15 minutes. The doctors wouldn't give me a C-section, even though there was an imminent danger of complications from preeclampsia. I was at high risk of bleeding to death due to my lack of platelets. My preeclampsia persisted after birth. I bled from nose, mouth, and the eyes, after giving birth. The personnel and the attending physician came once an hour to take blood samples. I received intravenous platelets through the arm, and some other form of medicine that I do not remember. I knew that I was very ill. The attending physician came once an hour to check on me, and samples of my blood were taken once per hour, throughout the day and night.

I was with my newborn son and was so happy; I also got to breast-feed him. At some point during the evening of the 11th February, I sat in my bed with pillows supporting my back. I had just breastfed my son and put him back in his crib. I began feeling very weak and ill; I also felt befuddled and dizzy. I had lost a lot of blood. I knew that when I lay down, I would die. At the time, I got that sense of "knowing" in a calm manner, without drama. I just noted the feeling. I tried all I could to remain sitting, but then I couldn't go on, and lay down in the bed.

Then I died. I, in silence and calm, slipped out of my body. I floated slowly and calmly out of my body from the back of my head, as if it was the most natural thing in the world. After floating under the ceiling, I left the room, leaving behind my body, my son sleeping by the bed in his crib, the hospital ward and the hospital.

After leaving the hospital, I arrived in some nice, very comforting and soft darkness. It felt so nice, soft and loving.

Then I saw a light very far away, but it came closer and closer while the soft and loving darkness pushed me towards the light. Then this unearthly, loving, and very beautifully radiating light surrounded me. In that overwhelming, radiating loving light, I met a glowingly beautiful and very loving being. It was as if I knew him (it was apparently a he). I knew then that I knew him, and felt completely comfortable and happy. His loving presence completely surrounded me. Together, we reviewed my life. All that I had experienced was done in a loving way, not in any judging way. My actions were observed, and all the feelings involved during the life were examined. Everything was and felt good to watch with him. While we were observing me with my good friend on earth, this light being joyously had an outbreak of light and loving messages about what good I had done in that moment we observed. We communicated with the use of our thoughts and mind.

There were a lot of smiles and happiness related with the review of my life, even though my life was not easy. My life had been tough, with many tears, betrayal, loneliness, abuse and more; but also, there was much joy with my grandparents and good playmates during my childhood, and later with my own children. All situations were examined, and all the good was emphasized and shown. I could see it with him; endure it all without feeling a single negative emotion attached to situations in my life. I was told what was especially good, including experiences where I had acted with my heart. In this way, I got to know what is especially good. Here is what I learned during the life review:

To be and act in love with the heart.

To be happy and be as good and pure in heart as possible with others.

Not to lie down, but to stand by myself and take care of myself.

Be true to my own values and myself.

To forgive without accepting negative actions from other, to let go and forgive.

To stay in joy.

To be in the present as much as possible.

To nourish myself.

To be my own best friend.

To be a good friend to others, and also remember that we all have our own path, to learn and work on accepting this.

To not brood over problems, but let go of them when it is difficult, and to address the challenges and problems again when I have the strength to overcome them.

To forgive myself and not push myself too much, to feel myself more and not cross my own limits and values.

To be good and honor ALL living things.

I learned that to die is so amazingly beautiful and full of joy and love.

It is strange when think about it now. There in my near-death experience, it didn't make me wonder. Almost nothing made me wonder and question events or the process of the life review throughout the near-death experience. Only much after, when I thought back, did I wonder about some of these experiences I had then.

I felt myself to be very awake and aware the whole time, I was immensely curious and observing, and my awareness was unearthly, much larger than we I am here in life. I could see 360 degrees around myself, I could focus on what I wanted to and it close-up without any problems, even without thinking about it. I could look up, down, forward and behind me all at once.

I felt more fresh and energized than ever, much more than when I am in life.

I had the feeling that I could do anything, not that I thought about it, but I had no problems at all, and never speculated on anything negative. I was energized, joyful and curious. I was there in the present moment, totally in the present. I felt no pain or gave it any thought.

At the same time I went through the life review, with all the emotions and experiences, together with this vibrant and very loving being who I just knew so well, without knowing from where, other than it must have been when I was in the afterlife, when I have been physically dead.

I was whole and totally safe.

Everything was sharper and I could focus on it when I wanted to, colors were clearer and vibrant. My field of view was all around. It was so beautiful and all the colors were unearthly beautiful. I was so happy and calm during all of my near-death experience.

I have hearing loss in my life on earth. However, I did not have that in death and I could hear much better than ever in my life. I had no trouble with my hearing; the sounds were beautiful and melodic. The conversations I had with others did not take place with sound, but rather with telepathy. I was completely filled with emotions, such as great joy; deep, deep love; comfort; gratitude; freedom; EVERYTHING-is-as-it-should-be feeling; All is well...

I got to know from the radiating being, my loving friend, that I was only on a visit here, and that I should return to my earthly life again. I didn't take this message in, and didn't pay attention to it, because I was occupied by everything else going on. I was paying attention to all that I got to know, everything that happened, and all the love and joy that I felt.

I was told that I would be divorced with my husband at the time, because we couldn't go on together. I was told that we both had something else to do on earth. My loving friend showed me that I should look at the divorce as a joyful thing for me, that it would give me joy and much freedom. But that it wasn't going to happen just yet. I was shown that I should forgive my husband, his actions and attitude. I was shown that even though he would hurt me deeply, this was part of my spiritual path for me to let go on him. Without this deep emotional hurt, I would never have been able leave him and go forward with my mission on earth. After the divorce, I was told that I should go forth with joy and gratitude throughout my earthly life. When I got sad after my NDE, then I should remember to focus on the joy, and to remember all the good that had happened in my life. This would heal my emotional wounds.

Life and love are processes on earth. There was much laughter, in a compassionate way, as he told me that I would find romantic love again and it would be like the dessert of the life. Right then I was shown how my soul mate looks, the one who would be my great love in the future, so that I could recognize him in the future when we meet. The reason that I was told this was to give me enough calm, so that I would work on myself, and on that life that I want to have. This gives me strength to know that this love will happen one day on earth.

I was also told that I would meet a lot of nice people, good friends and souls, so I should be looking forward to that. I would get to have many delightful experiences thereafter. I would begin to write and publish books about subjects I didn't know about yet. Then I learned that I would work with something completely different from what I had worked with up to then. I would have completely different goals in the future. I was told that I should take care of myself, my health, and be good to my body. , if I was that, I would be able to reach those goal I had set myself before I came into this life, and that it would give me so much happiness to reach these goals. That there were also great challenges ahead, which

I had set myself to overcome in this life, and that I should work on not letting it weigh me down, but rather take it in stride and with joy, and forgive myself if I didn't progress as quick as I wanted to. This learning process would give me great wisdom, understanding, and peace of mind to work through these problems. I was reminded to ask for help, because I would receive it. He said with laughter, "It is very important for you to learn that learning lessons will take its time." I felt very strongly that there is meaning to everything big that happens to us in our lives, including everything I experienced in my near-death experience. Events occurring in our lives on earth have meaning.

After the review of my past and future, I visited a very beautiful and lively landscape, where I had the experience of taking a walk with my energetic and radiating friend. All the colors were so beautiful and vibrant, as if everything was alive and buzzing. When we reached a beautiful spot, some souls came towards me. I recognized some of them. Everyone was so healthy and smiling. Those who had been old, looked at least 20 years younger. I saw my grandparents, all four of them who I loved so much in my life, were also there. They smiled and were quite happy. They gave me many hugs and much love. They told me that they had fun, were well, and they worked on whatever they desired the most. I also met several friends who had passed away. They had come to greet me, but ultimately, they all agreed that I had to go back since it wasn't my time yet.

I then met a group of souls who I didn't know from this life. But when I saw them, I just knew them deep in my soul. I knew them the best and cared most about them. I felt most connected with them in all of the universe! I was totally filled with happiness by the reunion, so much so that it felt like I cried of joy and surprise. I wondered why, in my 42 years I had lived on earth, that I had at not remembered them. It was overwhelming and indescribably wonderful to meet them.

Now that I look back upon the NDE, I can see that it wasn't all or just a bit of what happens in the afterlife that I saw there. What I saw and experienced, was specially arranged for me for my visit. I was at the same time so enveloped of the experience of this near-death experience that I didn't think about who I was or where I came from. Or for that matter, I wasn't worrying myself about anything. I didn't think about wanting to get back to my body. I only wanted to be right there, where I was. The experience completely took all my attention.

Suddenly a young man stood in front of me, and I knew that he also was my newborn son. He stared at me intensely. The he shouted throughout the place, "Mom, you promised me to be my mother in this life! Otherwise I wouldn't be here!" Immediately, I was propelled back to my body with immense speed. It only took a split-second to come back, and it hurt incredibly to get back in my body.

When I was leaving the hospital, the attending physician told me that I was that patient, who had been the most 'gone', and then came back again. He said that they couldn't do so much in that situation, other than give me plenty of platelets, watch me and then pray to God.

Was the kind of experience difficult to express in words? Yes. Some of the music and the colors that I saw and experienced do not exist here on Earth; they were unearthly. Some of the things I was shown, are difficult to describe because it doesn't exist here.

At the time of this experience, was there an associated life-threatening event? Yes. I died, and floated calmly out of my body. It was the most natural thing in the world. I floated up and under the ceiling. Then I left the room, my body, and the hospital.

How did your highest level of consciousness and alertness during the experience compare to your normal every day consciousness and alertness? More consciousness and alertness than normal.

If your highest level of consciousness and alertness during the experience was different from your normal every day consciousness and alertness, please explain: I felt very alert and fresh all the time. I was very curious while observing. My awareness was unearthly – much larger than when I am here in life. I could see 360 degrees around me; I could focus on what I wanted to look closer on without problems and without thought. I could look up, down, back and forth all at once.

Did your vision differ in any way from your normal, everyday vision (in any aspect, such as clarity, field of vision, colors, brightness, depth perception degree of solidity/transparency of objects, etc.)? Yes. I saw everything sharper, and could focus when I wanted to. The colors were much clearer and more vibrant than on earth. My field of view was 360 degrees. It was so beautiful; all colors were unearthly beautiful. I was so glad, happy and calm during the whole near-death experience.

Did your hearing differ in any way from your normal, everyday hearing (in any aspect, such as clarity, ability to recognize source of sound, pitch, loudness, etc.)? Yes. I have hearing loss in my life. I didn't have that in death. I heard much better than in life. I had no trouble with hearing; the sounds were nice and melodic. The conversations I had didn't use sound, but rather telepathy.

Did you experience a separation of your consciousness from your body? Yes.

What emotions did you feel during the experience? Great happiness. Deep, deep love. Well-being. Gratitude. Freedom. A feeling of all is as it should be. All is well.

Did you pass into or through a tunnel or enclosure? Yes. After I had left the hospital, I entered a pretty, comforting and soft darkness. It was soothing. There I saw a light very far away which came closer and closer, while the very soft darkness pushed me towards the light. Then I was immersed in this unearthly loving radiating light.

Did you see a light? Yes. After I had left the hospital, I entered a pretty, comforting and soft darkness. It was soothing. There I saw a light very far away which came closer and closer, while the very soft darkness pushed me towards the light, and then I was immersed in this unearthly loving radiating light.

Did you meet or see any other beings? Yes. In that overwhelming radiating loving light, I met a glowingly beautiful, very loving being. It was as if I knew him (it was apparently a he), I knew then that I knew him, and felt completely comfortable and happy. His loving presence completely surrounded me, and together we went try my life and all that I had experienced in a loving way, not any judging way. It was observed, and all the feelings involved during the life were examined. All events were, and felt, good to see with him. While we were observing something particularly good, my good friend came. This light being, with a kind of joy, had an outbreak of light while conveying loving messages about what good I had done in that moment we observed.

We communicated with the use of our thoughts and mind.

Did you experience a review of past events in your life? Yes. There were a lot of smiles and happiness related with the review of my life, even though my life was anything else than easy. It had been tough, with many tears, betrayal, loneliness, abuse and more. But also much joy with my grandparents and good playmates during my childhood, and later with my own children.

All situations were examined, and all the good was emphasized and shown. I could see it with him; endure it all without feeling a single negative emotion. I was told what actions were especially good, including experiences where I had acted with my heart without giving it any particular thought. In this way, I got to know what is especially good. To be and act in love from the heart.

Did you observe or hear anything regarding people or events during your experience that could be verified later? Yes. That I was only on a visit to the other side, and that I would have to go back again. I didn't really take this message in, and didn't take notice of it, as I was totally absorbed in all that was happening and all that love and happiness there.

I was told that I would get divorced later, because my husband and I couldn't walk on the same path anymore.

Also I was shown several of the place and houses I have lived in since then. I could recognize the houses when I saw them because they were shown to me in my near-death experience.

Did you see or visit any beautiful or otherwise distinctive locations, levels or dimensions? Yes. After the review of my past and future, I visited a very beautiful and lively landscape, where I had the experience of taking a walk with my energetic and radiating friend. All the colors were so beautiful and vibrant, as if everything was alive and buzzing. Here I reached a beautiful spot, where some souls came towards me, I recognized some of them.

Did you have any sense of altered space or time? Yes. Not that I have noticed it or thought about it. But the time has gone faster or I have been out of time, with all that I experienced, because I wasn't in our Earth time dead for very long.

Did you have a sense of knowing special knowledge, universal order and/or purpose? Yes. I felt very strong, and was absolutely sure that there is meaning to everything big that happens to us in our lives; including everything I experienced in my near-death experience, there is meaning in the lives we have.

Did you reach a boundary or limiting physical structure? No. I did not see, experience, or think of any boundary.

Did you become aware of future events? Yes and it fits completely with what happened later in my life.

Did you have any psychic, paranormal or other special gifts following the experience you did not have prior to the experience? Yes. I can remember many of my past lives now, about 100.

I have become more sensitive and more clairvoyant. I will often know when something happens, before it happens, both in my own life and on a global scale. I can see on other people, where they have lived in their past lives, and often what they have experienced.

I can feel other people's mood and energies, and recognize then. I can now also feel those who have passed away, and non-terrestrial beings.

Have you shared this experience with others? Yes. 4 years passed before I told anyone.

I did not know that near-death experiences existed when I had mine in 1996. I had never heard about it before. I was so happy when I discovered that other had experienced something similar to me. Then I told it to others, but not that many, only my closest friends. I have yet not met anyone who has had a near-death experience, but I have read about it, and read books about it.

I think it will be good to meet someone else who also had a near-death experience; I'm looking forward to meeting another NDEr someday. In the last 6 months of 2012, I began to talk about death to others as a therapist, since I have so powerful and joyful things to tell about death. I have learnt that I help others with their fear of death. When we release our fear of death, we get a more joyful life, no matter how many challenges we meet.

Did you have any knowledge of near death experience (NDE) prior to your experience? No.

How did you view the reality of your experience shortly (days to weeks) after it happened? Experience was definitely real. I knew that it was real at once, I just didn't know who to tell it about. I knew it was the truth and something I had really experienced. As soon as I was back in my body, I knew that the NDE was real and true, I have never doubted it. It is the truth.

Were there one or several parts of the experience especially meaningful or significant to you? Yes. My review of my life with the very caring and vibrant being, it was very significant. Especially the meeting with those I knew from this life, who had passed away, and I could see they were well, which gave me much joy. All that I was told about my future and what would happen. It was also significant when I had to go back to life again, because I knew of all the good experiences I had yet to have, and all the love I had yet to give and receive. The knowledge about some important events in the future, it was very significant for me to know. That I let go of my fear of death, and felt this unearthly wonderful love and happiness, that I remembered it again, because I remembered it as if I had been there before. It has helped me a lot after my near-death experience to know. It has totally changed my relationship with death, and to my life and how I relate to my fellow humans.

How do you currently view the reality of your experience? Experience was definitely real. My near-death experience is true. I have felt, saw and experienced it all and remember the NDE well. It is strong in my memory. That which I was told would happen in my future came true, and I couldn't have just imagined that. I knew the beings and people I had contact with in my near-death experience, also those I don't remember from this life, but who I immediately recognized as souls I knew deeply in my own soul. And even then in my near-death experience, I wondered why in so many years, 42 years, had not remembered them, that I had not remembered them at all in this life, before I met them on the other side of death, those I am the most connected in love with in the whole universe, those I love the most and deepest! I knew those I met in the most inner of my soul. I know it is reality. I know it is true.

Have your relationships changed specifically as a result of your experience? Yes. I prioritize other people's company in another way.

Material things are not important; the most important thing is interaction and experiences with other people. The most important is love at all levels, and to help others and myself where I can. It gives me great joy.

I'm now divorced from my husband, as he does not have the same values as I do now. I have become a very spiritual human.

Have your religious beliefs/practices changed specifically as a result of your experience? Yes. I was before my near-death experience very politically active in the left-wing of Danish politics, and didn't think much of religious matters. I knew that life didn't end with death, but didn't think more about it. I was busy with politics, work and being mother to 9 children. I had enough things to take care of, and to make a good life for my children.

I now know that there is a life after death. I now know that there is no hell other than the one we create ourselves. I know the most important thing is love between people and all beings. I know that we are here to learn and reflect in each other. I know that I receive as much help from the other side, as I am ready to receive, from those who I am most connected to in love.

I now know that those are passed away sometimes visits me and follows me in what happens in my life.

I now know that I have set myself for something good, that I will reach in this life.

I now know that all my children have chosen me as a mother, in love.

I now know that I am loved.

I now know that I am here in this life for among other things, to learn to love myself.

I now know that there is a meaning with it all, why we are here.

Following the experience, have you had any other events in your life, medications or substances which reproduced any part of the experience? No.

Is there anything else you would like to add concerning the experience? I am now so grateful for the near-death experience I had. It has changed me to a much happier and aware human being. I have other values. I am so grateful for the knowledge I have now. It is a great gift to me to know all about death and all the loving souls on the other side. It is comforting to know that these souls want the best for me, my family and all those in life on this Earth. I am honored to have experienced this supernatural wonderful love and happiness that exists.

I am so grateful to have this gift of remembering many, many past lives of my own, terrible, fun, strange, serious and very loving experiences. I now see everything from a bigger perspective, I know there is a meaning with all that I have experienced, and that I have had a big influence on what I experienced in all my past lives, and in my current life. It is a great gift to get an understanding of wholeness. I have gotten my universal understanding through my NDE and the special abilities I got after my experience. I can remember past lives and some of my in-between lives.

I now have a much better understanding of my childhood and my life, and I can see it all in a greater perspective. It allows me to know the overshadowing great love that exists. It allows me to know my best soul-friends who wait on me on the other side, and I know they help me as much as they can, when I remember to ask for help, which I often forget to do.

Did the questions asked and information you provided so far accurately and comprehensively describe your experience? Yes. I did the best I could, maybe I have forgotten some details, but all in all is the most important for others to know. I remember messages about me, my life and my future that I have not written about here, because they are only about me.

Though I can say that everything which I have been told would happen in my life, did happen, beside that which lies in the future.

Not that I always have remembered it, but when it then happened, I then remembered that I was told about this on the side in my near-death experience. This happened for example with my divorce.

I still work on some of my old habits, so I can become even more in the present and in joy. But it will take the time it takes, even though I received guidance in my near-death experience about it being important that I do it.

Are there any other questions we could ask to help you communicate your experience? I want to think about that; it is so new to me to share my experiences with others.

SIX

John's NDE has two components that we often see in NDEs. The easiest to describe is the intense anger that many feel at returning to their bodies. When they are in such a beautiful, loving place, it is hard to return to earth.

The other aspect that we see has to do with relatives. Even in the after death communication website (www.adcrf.org), where the loved ones from the other side contact the living on earth with a message, there is a higher than normal contact and meetings with blood relatives. This is suggestive that the very DNA in our physical bodies not only connects us to our relatives on earth, but also in the hereafter. Another aspect of NDE is that it is not uncommon for people to meet relatives they didn't know on earth. His nephew was the age he would have been had he lived. Many times a loved one will appear in radiant health and at an optimum time in their lives when they felt alive and vibrant. Other times, they will maintain the age and form they were on earth because it is the one that is most easily recognized by the experiencer.

JOHN V.

I was in treatment for stage 4 Non-Hodgkin's Lymphoma. I was home and in tremendous pain. The doctors told me to put my life in order; they had given me a one in four chance to live.

I started to pray, "God, please take me." I felt my pain stop and I found myself looking down at myself. Suddenly, I found myself in a musty smelling environment. It was scary. At the end of the tunnel was a brilliant light. I walked toward the light and then into another world. Heaven? There was a point where I couldn't go any further.

I saw my grandmother who had died when I was a teenager. She was crying, with her arms held out to hug me. When we hugged, it was like getting out of a cold lake and your mother would wrap a warm towel around you. I had a feeling of total unconditional love. I had no pain, just a feeling of total wellness. While hugging her, I realized we were floating. I could see people waving to me like they were welcoming me home. At this point, my grandmother spoke to me in Polish as she did when I was growing up. She told me how sorry she was that I was sick, but that I had to go back and finish my life. Then, a young man appeared. He resembled my nephew Michael, who had died in a car accident. But, it wasn't him. He said his name was "Steven." I had never met him.

In an instant, I was back in my body. My wife was holding her hands over me and praying aloud. I didn't tell her what had happened.

It took me about two years to talk to my wife about what I had experienced. She told me that she thought I had left her. She also told me that I was very angry when I woke up. I began to tell her what I had seen. I saw such vivid colors that all my senses were stimulated. I then told her about the young man, Steven, that I had met. When I told her he looked like my nephew Michael but slightly older, she started to cry. Two years before my nephew Michael was born, my sister had a stillborn baby boy. What I didn't know is, they had named him Steven. This was to me the proof that what I had experienced was real.

At the time of your experience was there an associated life-threatening event? Yes. I had stage 4 cancer.

Was the experience difficult to express in words? Yes. I didn't think anyone would believe me.

At what time during the experience were you at your highest level of consciousness and alertness? More consciousness and alertness than normal. After coming out of the tunnel and experiencing the vivid colors and sound.

Please compare your vision during the experience to your everyday vision that you had immediately prior to the time of the experience. I have poor eyesight normally. There, you are whole and can see perfectly.

Please compare your hearing during the experience to your everyday hearing that you had immediately prior to the time of the experience. Same as with eyesight, I could hear perfectly.

Did you see or hear any earthly events that were occurring during a time that your consciousness/awareness was apart from your physical/earthly body? No.

What emotions did you feel during the experience? Totally loved.

Did you pass into or through a tunnel? Yes. The tunnel was dark and musty smelling but the light at the end was bright and was pulling me toward it.

Did you see an unearthly light? Uncertain - just brilliant.

Did you seem to encounter a mystical being or presence, or hear an unidentifiable voice? No

Did you encounter or become aware of any deceased (or alive) beings? Yes. Grandmother and nephew.

Did you become aware of past events in your life during your experience? Yes. My life past before my eyes

Did you seem to enter some other, unearthly world? A clearly mystical or unearthly realm - the door of heaven.

Did time seem to speed up or slow down? Everything seemed to be happening at once; or time stopped or lost all meaning. Everything was so wonderful you could see and experience everything seemingly at once.

Did you suddenly seem to understand everything? No.

Did you reach a boundary or limiting physical structure? Yes. It was a feeling that I couldn't go any farther.

Did you come to a border or point of no return? I came to a barrier that I was not permitted to cross; or was "sent back" against my will. I was told it wasn't my time and that I had a life to finish.

Did scenes from the future come to you? No.

Did you have a sense of knowing special knowledge or purpose? Uncertain.

Discuss any changes that might have occurred in your life after your experience. Large changes in my life. I used to be a very busy person. I had many acquaintances, but now I have friends. I try to be as caring to people as I can. I understand that money will mean nothing someday but the kind of person I was on earth will mean everything.

Did you have any changes in your values or beliefs after the experience that occurred as a result of the experience? Yes.

Do you have any psychic, non-ordinary or other special gifts after your experience that you did not have before the experience? No.

Have you ever shared this experience with others? Yes. It took two years to tell my wife. A year later I told sister, who is the mother of the nephew I met. It is a comforting feeling to everyone I tell. People are genuinely interested in the afterlife.

Did you have any knowledge of near death experience (NDE) prior to your experience? Yes. Just what you would read or hear about.

What did you believe about the reality of your experience shortly (days to weeks) after it happened? Experience was definitely real. I know what I experienced, I'll never forget it and I selfishly can't wait to return.

What do you believe about the reality of your experience at the current time? Experience was definitely real.

Have your relationships changed specifically as a result of your experience? Yes. I try to surround myself with good people. Not everyone believes me about my experience, but that's ok. As long as they are a good person, they will find out for themselves someday.

Have your religious beliefs/spiritual practices changed specifically as a result of your experience? Yes. I don't believe in one kind of religion anymore.

At any time in your life, has anything ever reproduced any part of the experience? No.

Did the questions asked and information that you provided accurately and comprehensively describe your experience? Yes.

Are there one or several parts of your experience that are especially meaningful or significant to you? Meeting my nephew who died at birth.

SEVEN

The first experience is a probable NDE because she was only age three at the time and it is hard to tell if the experience happened at the same time as the asthma attack. However, the experience itself makes it highly probable that this was a NDE. I included this as typical of what we see as a child NDE. Zena has vivid recall of the memory even though she couldn't put it into words at the time of the experience. Her memory of the event was so clear, that she could describe relatives that she had never seen before and her father could tell her who she saw by the descriptions she gave. Again, there is the aspect of seeing blood relatives, such as in John's experience. Child NDErs show that the NDE occurs and that it is not dependent on age, culture, religion, or ethnicity. NDEs occurring at such a young age are evidence of the reality of NDEs.

When asked, "Did you experience anything on earth that reproduced the NDE?" most people answer "No" to this question. Of the few that answer "Yes," the top two answers are: 1) another NDE, or 2) remembrance of the NDE.

ZENA M.

OK, I have to go at this backwards, since I didn't know anything about "it" until I was 16.

I was 16 and my Dad and I were on a long drive together - just the two of us. We were talking about all kinds of things. I told him about a really strange 'dream' I'd had years and years ago, and couldn't understand how it had remained so vivid for all these years.

I told him that I had walked down a dim hallway. At the end was a door that was just a tiny bit open. There was lovely, bright sunlight coming from the bit of open doorway. When I pushed it open, there was a green lawn or field in front of me. There was a stream with a little bridge over it. On the other side of the bridge were all these people who obviously knew me, as they called me by my family nickname and greeted me warmly. I did not know any of these people.

As I started to enter the place, there was a bright, bright (but soft) light shaped like if you drew an oval around a person. It came from nowhere and although there was no sense of being touched (except by love), I moved backwards out the door. The light said to me, "Not yet." And the door shut.

I felt a very sharp sense of regret and loss, but didn't know why or for what - as much as a child of three can conceptualize those emotions. Anyway, when I finished telling my dad about the 'dream' he said to me "That would have been when you died." He explained to me about the asthma attack.

He also then told me he knew many of the people I described. He told me that I had been 'dead' for approximately 45 minutes from an asthma attack when I was age three. He said that I was returned to life by the prayers of the practitioner they had called.

Being a typical teenager I just said "Dead? Are you sure?" (Even in the 1960s, we didn't trust our parents to really know much about anything)

He replied to me "I was a medic in the Army. I know dead when I see it."

He warned me not to ask my mother about it. Back then, no one talked about things like that or they'd locked you up in a mental institution. So, I really haven't talked about it, but it has remained very much a part of my earthly experience. We never spoke of it again.

At the time of your experience was there an associated life-threatening event? Uncertain. It was an asthma attack, and I guess that can be considered life threatening?

Was the experience difficult to express in words? Uncertain. I'm not certain there really are words to adequately describe the feelings I had during an experience like that. Although, I was so young when it happened, I was still pre-literate so feelings were, maybe, more central to my everyday experience and maybe more 'familiar'? I'm not even sure what exactly I'm trying to say here, except that when it happened, it all seemed so normal and natural except for the sense of love enveloping me from the light and the quite poignant sense of regret when I had to leave, which I didn't understand at all.

At what time during the experience were you at your highest level of consciousness and alertness? Normal consciousness and alertness. I have absolutely NO memory of anything before or after what I have described above, and the whole experience there seemed to be at the same level of awareness.

Please compare your vision during the experience to your everyday vision that you had immediately prior to the time of the experience. I was three - I don't know for sure, but nothing seemed extraordinary at all.

Did you see or hear any earthly events that were occurring during a time that your consciousness/awareness was apart from your physical/earthly body? No.

What emotions did you feel during the experience? For most of it, nothing unusual. I was a kind of solitary kid who lived in the country, so was always wandering off exploring and having the whole community out searching for me. Therefore, this seemed like just another interesting walk. Children did that in those days. I went outside to play and went to the fields and woods and could be gone for several hours before anyone got concerned.

Did you pass into or through a tunnel? Uncertain. My experience was a hallway as opposed to a tunnel.

Did you see an unearthly light? Yes. Adult-sized oval "cloud" lit from within, or maybe it was the light itself. This is really hard to explain.

Did you seem to encounter a mystical being or presence, or hear an unidentifiable voice? I encountered a definite being, or a voice clearly of mystical or unearthly origin. The light was "alive" and seemed to have - individuality or personhood - but was still light and it glowed not really from within, but in its entirety.

It spoke to my thoughts, not to my ears, so maybe I shouldn't call it a voice, yet that's what it seemed like. All it said was, "Not yet."

Did you encounter or become aware of any deceased (or alive) beings? Yes. Ok, taking into account my age at the time, and even as I view it in retrospect, they were PEOPLE, not beings.

I didn't know them, but they knew me and welcomed me using my family nickname. Even at age 16, all those years later, I could describe them with such detail and accuracy that my father recognized most of them. They were relatives who had passed on before I was even born. I'd never met these relatives and we had no photographs of them.

Did you become aware of past events in your life during your experience? No.

Did you seem to enter some other, unearthly world? Some unfamiliar and strange place. Well, the dim hallway led to a door which was slightly ajar. Bright light was coming from the opening in the doorway and I pushed the door open.

Inside was a green space, immediately in front of the door - a large lawn or closely mown field. Some distance across the grass, was a stream with a little bridge over it. Beyond the bridge were the people seemingly waiting for me.

Did time seem to speed up or slow down? No.

Did you suddenly seem to understand everything? No. These concepts don't seem relevant to the experience of a 3 yr. old.

Did you reach a boundary or limiting physical structure? Yes. The door way was open when I went to it, but when I was 'pushed' out, the door closed - a very definite barrier.

Did you come to a border or point of no return? I came to a barrier that I was not permitted to cross; or was "sent back" against my will. I was 3. Children in those days weren't allowed to have "will" where any difference with adults was concerned, but I did feel a sense of loss but didn't know for what, and regret to be leaving.

Did scenes from the future come to you? No.

Did you have a sense of knowing special knowledge or purpose?
No.

Discuss any changes that might have occurred in your life after your experience. Large changes in my life.

Did you have any changes in your values or beliefs after the experience that occurred as a result of the experience? Yes. Over many decades, after I found out what happened, I went looking for something to explain it, and tried to find something that would make me feel that way again. So while my values remained fairly constant, my beliefs have shifted all over the map trying to find what it felt like I'd lost. Not sure if this is what you want? Oh, and I've ALWAYS looked at death as just stepping into another room because of that experience.

Do you have any psychic, non-ordinary or other special gifts after your experience that you did not have before the experience? Uncertain. Gave messages at a Spiritualist Temple for a while, did some readings for people after I was involved with Santa Ria for a while, had some dreams such as that my son was going to get hit by a car, which he was the next day, had some out-of-body experiences (at least one validated).

I found these things interesting for a while, but basically worthless. One thing I was very sure of because of this experience and what was validated during the 'psychic' part of my life, is that personality remains unchanged after the event we call death. I felt that I was harming the progress of many that called on me to help them cope, as many didn't want to move on with their own development.

In later years, many times when I had an asthma attack, I would return to the same hallway. I never went to the end door again, but there were also side doors. One time when I was a bit older, I went in one of the side doors and a being (as opposed to a person) explained to me that there was a big flaw in what we thought we knew about mathematics and showed me how it was correctly done. I don't remember a thing about the explanation, but up to Grade 10, I got almost perfect marks in mathematics and tested out as a mathematical genius apparently.

Have you ever shared this experience with others? Yes. My experience was around 1949. I first shared it about 1962 - and that's when I actually found out what happened. The reaction was atypical for the times as I was actually told what happened, but typical in the sense that I knew it was not something to be talked about. Haven't ever really talked about it in detail much though have mentioned it briefly when people were discussing death. Think maybe I've told the whole story to maybe two people in my life since the first discussion.

Did you have any knowledge of near death experience (NDE) prior to your experience? No.

What did you believe about the reality of your experience shortly (days to weeks) after it happened? Experience was definitely not real. I had always believed it was just a really vivid dream as I was too young to remember being sick or any of the before and after details.

What do you believe about the reality of your experience at the current time? Experience was definitely real. Well, it was so vivid, and being able to describe people I'd never seen who had passed on (My father was no airy-fairy kind of guy. He was very realistic, common sense-like and grounded), and the whole "stepping into another room" view of death that it gave me (which kind of seems like a sensible way for things to work) . . . the first two reasons made it seem credible then (when I was told the story) and the last reason kind of buttressed the belief.

Have your relationships changed specifically as a result of your experience? Yes. After I found out about what had happened, it kind of went a long way to explaining why my mom kept me on such a short leash compared to the other kids in the area. But that's probably not what you want.

Have your religious beliefs/spiritual practices changed specifically as a result of your experience? Yes. After learning about what happened, it led to a 50 year search to try and find the meaning and the feeling again, only to end up back where I started.

At any time in your life, has anything ever reproduced any part of the experience? Yes. A couple of other asthma attacks as a child took me part way down the hall, but never got to the door again.

More than two decades later I had (another long story, sorry) some kind of reaction to a barbiturate sleeping pill. After you take one, there is a short episodes of being awake and kind of hypnotized into thinking that you've never been asleep so you take more. Anyway, that happened. I finished the sleeping pills - I only had one more, but then apparently took 23 other kinds of leftover pills I had lying around, (I'm the original packrat) stuff for everything from itchy skin to migraine.

(Another NDE) At one of the lucid periods, I saw the empty pill bottles and managed to call my brother, who came over (he could tell there was trouble as I passed out again while on the phone and dropped it and me). He couldn't get an answer at my door so he called the police and they broke in. The police did what they could and I was taken to hospital in an ambulance. I remember 'seeing' myself in a small room with three doctors and they were using the paddles on my chest (I had the burns to verify that part). I was sitting 'up there' somewhere watching them and thinking, "Please, just leave me alone! It's so peaceful like this." And then they did. One doctor shrugged and they turned off the machine, turned, and walked away. AS they walked away, a voice said "If you stay, your ex-husband will get to raise the kids." That was not an option. I rejoined my body on the table so hard, it rattled and the doctors turned around again - and that's all I remember until I regained consciousness in a more normal way.

Did the questions asked and information that you provided accurately and comprehensively describe your experience? Yes. If you take into account the extra explanations, I made in the wrong boxes when there were questions that needed enlarged answers. I think that due to the age I was when it actually happened, I didn't quite fit into all the boxes properly.

Are there one or several parts of your experience that are especially meaningful or significant to you? Mine was seemingly so short, but everything after I opened the door became very meaningful after I was old enough to understand the concepts and was told what happened. Knowing that I was still me, and the other people there were still them gave me a sense of death as nothing to be feared, but also nothing to be sought, as in the words of an old country song "Wherever you go, there you are."

EIGHT

Cherie is from South Africa. Her experience imparts a lot of wisdom and hope. What I love about this experience is that it shows that even though she has many hardships on earth, there is a purpose for her life – and she chose to come back to resolve her prior lifetimes of unresolved emotions and fears. Another important concept has to do with her description of heaven, hell and purgatory as different states of consciousness. I appreciate her description of viewing her earthly life from the perspective of the other side; that there is universal timing that shows itself in a synchronous chain of events.

CHERIE B.

Within minutes of arriving in the emergency room of my local hospital, I went into cardiac arrest. I hadn't been feeling well for about three weeks but no one could figure out what was medically going on. I had symptoms of shortness of breath, chest pain, and now I was complaining to my husband that my arms felt heavy. At that point, he had no choice but to take me back to the emergency room of my local hospital, just as he had done a few weeks prior.

Emergency medical staff came rushing to my side to begin administering Cardio-Pulmonary Resuscitation (CPR). My heart would restart and then flat line again. This went on for nearly ninety-minutes until the medical team began preparing to call my time of death for the death certificate. As each critical second passed, my local Cardiologist, who had known me for several years now and happened to be on-call that day, refused to give up. He instructed the doctors and nurses to continue with CPR long enough to install lifesaving support systems to provide oxygen to my organs. It was unclear at this point, if there was any damage to my brain.

If there were any hope for my survival, it would be one of the top hospitals for Cardio-Thoracic Care in the country. It was then that arrangements were made to end me. The ambulance rushed me to New York City where some of the world's top surgeons would miraculously save me. It took several open-heart surgeries, the latest in advanced biomedical technology, and over four critical and grueling months to survive. While all of this was happening to my physical body, something interesting happened to my spirit. After falling instantly into a coma when I first went into cardiac arrest, my consciousness traveled to a world I had never seen before. This is where my journey into the afterlife begins.

All of the sudden, I found myself drifting. I called out to a friend of mine, who I had visited the day before. I couldn't see her, but I could feel her presence. I asked her, "Where am I?" Then I remembered something she had said to me earlier. She told me that sometimes in life we are given a choice of whether we want to stay on this side or go back to earth. At the time, I didn't know what she was referring to. She explained a little further. A friend of hers who experienced what I was now experiencing had to decide if her soul wanted to go home or not. Home referred to her heavenly home. Her friend made the choice to go home. I was still confused as to why she was telling me all this and how it related to me. I was terrified of death and dying, so I surely wasn't ready to transition on.

It was really quiet. I didn't see much, but I was in an unfamiliar state. I felt as light as a feather, as if I was floating in air. It also felt as if I no longer had a physical body. I called out to my friend in a gentle voice, as if she was standing right next me. I said, "Oh, is this what you meant by making a choice of whether or not to come back?" I instantly knew something had happened to me and that I had died. I remember thinking how easy of a transition it was. One minute you could be alive and the next minute you could instantly be in a whole other world. I thought, "That's it? That's all you have to do when you die?" I was amazed at how much fear I always had around death. Yet there I was, floating around in this beautiful, light space where I felt safe and whole. The overwhelming beauty felt so wonderful. For the first time I could remember, I felt free and at peace.

Suddenly, I found myself deep within the beautiful ocean floors. The various hues of colors were breathtaking. They were vivid and more beautiful than I had ever seen. I was floating effortlessly and soon found myself surrounded by a circle of beings floating all around me. They had the form of a human but were dressed in all black and looked similar to a scuba free diver. Their suits extended over their faces so I was unable to see any facial features. They all looked the same and were about twenty feet away, all in a circle surrounding me. I felt no fear but was frustrated that none of them was saying anything to me. It felt like they were just staring at me. I never felt threatened, but I wasn't quite sure what to make of the situation. I said to them, "I know what happened, I know why I am here, can you please take me to the light so I can go home and enjoy the rest of my days in this beautiful place?"

I had suffered so much in this lifetime and felt that I had disappointed so many people. I was ready to move on and make my transition. But there was no response from my new circle of friends. I was getting really frustrated.

I then thought about my husband and my family. I wondered if I should return to them. But it felt better letting them move on with their lives, without the burden of my life to worry about. I knew it would be hard on them at first, but that it would be easier in the long run, since something terrible must have happened to my body. I felt free in my decision. For some reason I was sure they would all be okay without me. I felt so connected to everything here - so safe, and so loved. I was free and I wanted to set my family free too.

So without hesitation, I asked again to be taken to the light. Something then gave me the sense that they didn't want me to rush into my decision. It must have been shortly thereafter that I found myself in a whirlwind of non-linear time and space.

I began to experience a series of events that all seemed to have a similar theme. It felt as if I was getting glimpses of past karmic energy that continued to follow me into different lifetimes. I had experiences with loved ones who had passed on, such as my grandmother and a long-time family friend. I even had experiences with loved ones who are currently still alive. I experienced interaction with beings who I didn't know as well. I interacted with beings who had form and non-form. There was no order to these events and sometimes they appeared to be happening all at the same time. There was one event in which I witnessed my own funeral and for some reason it repeated at least three times over and over, similar to the movie Groundhog Day.

Some of the events I experienced were beautiful and some were very traumatic and still to this day, difficult to talk about. I found myself drifting endlessly throughout a mysterious realm, not knowing when it would all end.

But there was a point during this series of events, in which I had changed my mind about leaving my family. I remember saying that I wanted to return to my family and that I no longer wanted to be taken to the light. I had decided that if I returned, I could work out these long-held karmic energies with the family and friends whom I knew and loved. I remember missing my family and urgently wanting to see them again.

Suddenly, I found myself being taken up a mountain in a car and seeing this beautiful and glistening mansion compound off in the far distance. When we arrived, I was placed in one of the rooms. The walls, the bed, the sheets, and the clothing everyone was wearing, all of it was white. I was placed on a white table in this small room. It was quiet and I was alone. Every so often, someone would come to check on me and I would ask when I could leave. No one ever said anything to me, but it was implied that I was to remain as long as my body needed to heal.

After a very long and frustrating wait, I began a rebirth process. I experienced another set of various events in which I had to struggle to be removed from water. I had never breathed air before, so anytime I was removed from water, I would suffocate and had to be submerged back under the water. This seemed to go on forever. It felt as traumatic as it must feel for a baby being born and taking its first breath of air. Eventually, my brother was able to safely transition me out of the water. At this point, I found myself awake from my coma with my brother, who had flown in from across the country, standing right by my side.

It had been almost a week since I had first fallen into my coma and I was still in critical care. I had endured open-heart surgery and was connected to a mechanical heart and lung machine. Shortly thereafter, I was placed back into my coma. I endured another six to eight weeks of surgeries with severe complications. Everyone was concerned whether or not I would survive.

I didn't begin sharing my experience until a few years after I had finally returned home. My recovery was grueling and it took a very long time for me to physically and emotionally process everything I had experienced. I wasn't familiar with the term Near Death Experience

(NDE) so I really didn't know what to think of my travels through consciousness. It was a very confusing time for me.

To pass some of the time during my recovery, I began to write. I would write endlessly every day, whatever came to my mind. I started to write about my experiences on the other side that I was unable to share with anyone. Before I knew it, I had three hundred pages of everything that had been trapped inside my head since the incident.

It wasn't until a friend of mine forwarded a story of a lady who had been on the verge of death and had a very similar experience to me, that I finally realized there were others who understood and experienced something similar to what I had gone through.

A year later, I found the courage to start sharing my story as well.

There are so many lessons about life that I learned throughout my journey in the after-realm. I learned how vast the realm of consciousness is and that we are only participating in a fragment of all that is possible. I learned that there is a much bigger picture in how the world works than what we see on earth. We have only cracked the surface of discovery. I learned how much of our earthly lives are run on fear and that sometimes things happen in life that just cannot be explained in our current frame of reference.

Time did not seem to exist as we currently define it - it felt more non-linear than linear. The concept of Heaven seemed to be more a state of consciousness than an actual place we go to when we pass on. What we refer to as Hell appeared to be more of a state of consciousness, only it consisted of unresolved emotions and fears that follows us throughout many lifetimes. Purgatory also seemed to exist, again more as a state of consciousness, in which beings were lost because loved ones had not yet let them go or because they themselves had unresolved emotions to work through.

Most importantly, I learned, that our consciousness appears to continue even after the body has ceased to function. It was a very powerful awakening for me. My life has never been the same. I look at the world through new eyes, filled with awe and wonder. And the fear that had dictated every move and decision of my earthly life, seemed to ease and release its hold on me.

I am often asked if I have any psychic, paranormal, or other special gifts following my NDE, that I did not have prior to the experience. I feel that we all have these special gifts, whether we are aware of them or not, but it does appear that my abilities have been heightened since my experience.

It took me a very long time to understand what I had experienced during my journey throughout the afterlife, but over time, it has all come together for me in a powerful message about life, love, hope, and possibilities.

Since my cardiac arrest, I have begun to realize how many amazing signs had appeared to me either over the years or very shortly before it happened. These signs are a set of coincidences that played out synchronicity like an orchestra of life.

A little over ten years ago, I had a dream that I was having open-heart surgery. Then, a few weeks prior to my cardiac arrest, I began making what felt like preparations such as cleaning up my belongings, closing social media accounts, and resigning from my post as member of the Board of Directors for a non-profit corporation in South Africa. Just two days prior, I sent a text to my friend saying, "I think I'm dying". One day prior, I visited my friend who had told me that sometimes we are given a choice of whether or not we want to stay or go. The night before my cardiac arrest, right before my husband fell asleep; I looked at my dog and then said to my husband, "Promise me you will take care of my boy if something happens to me." He said to me, "I already told you a long time ago that I would." I eagerly replied, "I know, but I need you to say it again." My husband then said, "I promise I will take care of him", and then drifted off to sleep. That was my last memory.

Although I have never been raised under a specific religion, I have always been a curious individual. I was curious about life and what happens when we die. Ultimately, my experience confirmed my own belief in survival of our consciousness and that we are never alone, even after our physical body ceases to exist.

Most of my relationships have changed since my NDE, mostly because I have changed. Most of my relationships have become stronger with time and some have drifted away. Some are still struggling with the fear of almost losing me in their life.

There are only a few things in my life, which have been able to reproduce the expansiveness of what I experienced during my NDE, but without a doubt, nature is the place I go to the most to reconnect with my experience of the other side.

As I share my story, I am continuously reminded that everyone and everything is exactly as it should be. For whatever reason, I am still here. It is my hope that in sharing my story I can help to inspire others to open possibilities for their lives, help those who are grieving loved ones who had passed on, and assist medical researchers in the topic of the survival of our soul and whether or not consciousness continues after our physical body ceases to exist.

Despite the challenging road this has been for me, my journey has been nothing less than a miracle and I am eternally grateful for the sacred journey I was blessed to have experienced.

NINE

Yazmine is from New Zealand. Her account shows just how ineffable her experience was. Many times she struggles for the right word or set of words, but the words still do not describe what she experienced. She experiences the OBE state and watches as the nurses try to bring her back to life. She can feel their emotions and sense their thoughts. This is known as veridical perception. Then she leaves this realm and has a detailed life review. Yazmine describes the matrix of love that is the fabric of the universe. She calls this the Serene Goldenness. She does not use the name "God" to describe the creator or supreme being of the universe; rather, she feels that the "Great Presence" is more appropriate. Even now, Yazmine is still connected to the other side. She continues to operate on earth with a different state of consciousness due to experiencing altered awareness from the other side. This is also characteristic of many NDErs, especially those who have a deep experience.

YAZMINE S.

I miscarried the baby in the hospital. Although I was very sad about the event, I felt that there was a greater reason for the experience as it was all part of a divine plan by The Great Presence.

Two nurses accompanied me as we went upstairs for an internal exam. As we went up, I felt myself begin to reel backwards.

As I lost consciousness, I left my body. I went round and round through space. I stopped spinning and then began flying past planets and stars. I flew through the rings of Saturn, seeing massive rocks and dust particles right before my eyes. I was marveling at the astounding beauty and laughing about how no one on Earth would believe this! It all felt so wonderful and so exactly perfect. I was an astronaut, a fabulous free spirit of joy! I was filled with indescribable joy and love for all of creation from the vastness of space to the smallest of all nano-expressions!

Suddenly, the scene changed and I was back in the hospital. I was lying on a stretcher bed, wearing a white hospital gown, I looked at my body and knew it wasn't the real me. It was the shell that my soul had been caught inside, and now I was free! Oh and how I felt such happiness! The joy was all-pervasive. My body represented the real world, pain, suffering, and loss. All of the earth experience was illusionary. It was like I was so involved in the earthly experience, that I couldn't see the amazing wonder, beauty and joy that was truly my real world. Everything was becoming clear to me.

The nurses were calling my name. One nurse was crying tears, while the other was saying, "Oh my God, we've lost her!" Meanwhile, I was above them thinking what silly-billies they were for making all that fuss. I was also wondering why they couldn't see me and why they didn't realize that all was perfectly fabulous!

Then I saw a window that was opened about 6 inches wide. I thought, "Wow, I wonder if I can fit through there?" Then instantly I was in another dimension. I was flying through Goldenness that was pure, serene, and delightful. I was held by this Serene Goldeness for the longest time. I couldn't do anything except be with It. It was with me, It was inside me, It was me. It had always been in and with everything. It was and is Truth, Love, Compassion, Joy, and the All. This Goldenness held all information. It was the One Mind. It contained the creation of all of everything ever created.

I felt and experienced everything that has ever been and ever shall be. Everything is simultaneously occurring. There is no past or future. It all just IS. There is no way to describe the immaculate beauty of this experience, though every day for the last 35 years I wish I could find a way. Bliss is a mere descriptive word, yet does not say what I wish I explained. Yes, bliss is a close word - sort of.

I saw and experienced every single detail of my present life up to that moment. It was like watching a movie, yet simultaneously, I was starring as the main character simultaneously. Watching my life made me feel quite sad because I had not lived my life in a state of serene joy. I felt ashamed that I had not realized how imperative it is for one to be incredibly happy in this life. The challenge is to be happy the pain, fear, or no matter the circumstances.

In this natural state of ultimate freedom and blissful awareness, all the material conflicts of body and mind are quite unimportant. I felt that I had been unfaithful to The Great Presence, who like a Divinely loving Mother, I had let down. I was my own judge. Yet, I was this Love simultaneously. I saw how all of Humanity has walked with their eyes cast low to the Earth, not opening wide to the beauty of the One loving presence of Golden peace. This is where we truly live, but yet do not see. I saw how sadness overcomes those who cannot forgive themselves or others.

I was shown that by being uplifted, we could all ascend to true joy together as a loving family of Beings beyond the human life of mundane ness. I saw how there is a level of fear so ingrained in some people. That was hard for me to see. Yet I also saw that they too could find a way through to this world of peacefulness. I saw how things would change only after massive suffering; yet there remained the possibility to end suffering. I saw that I had a purpose and that all beings have purpose. I saw that we are not separate; we are all the One. And I saw that we must have all the courage possible to achieve this fabulous unity. It is highly possible.

I felt and experienced all of creation as an omni-experience. There was no time involved at any level. I saw that creation is so simple that it cannot be expressed. It is best to let the mind be still and then it may occur of itself. It was such a feeling of raised joy that I was in. In the distance, a Great Presence appeared. This Presence is the most Ultimate of Holiness, emanating with extraordinary Brilliance! This Great Presence is the Heart of all.

When I put my arms out to fly, I saw that they were rainbows of colors. I was a rainbow being, made of light and exquisite color. I was overjoyed! I thought that I can fly to the Great Presence and unite with the purity of all that is was and ever shall be. That was my heart's desire. I wanted to be at one with the Great Presence, which most call "God," and yet I dare not announce a name to that which is beyond naming.

I begin to fly and move closer to that beauteous sight. I began to feel the Great Presence pervade my very core being, as if my entirety was exploding into love. Then I heard a great, powerful voice, which seemed to echo in all directions. It vibrated through to my very soul. I hear, "It is not your time." Upon hearing this, I feel such sorrow. In my mind I am saying, "No, no, no! Please don't make me go back. I do not want to return to this Earth, ever again."

Two days later, I woke up in the hospital bed. I started to cry as I felt the heartache that I am here on Earth again. I have never felt at home here. I feel so alone because I struggle to find anyone to connect and to share my experience with. I feel like I have been living a double life. The life on earth while secretly still connected to the other side.

At the time of your experience was there an associated life-threatening event? Yes. I had a miscarriage when I was 5 months pregnant. While I laid in bed overnight, I almost bled to death. The staff had to give me 6 pints of blood. I was 'out' or 'dead' for 6 minutes, then remained unconscious for two days.

Was the experience difficult to express in words? Yes. To explain the VASTNESS of PURE JOY and WISDOM is impossible!

At what time during the experience were you at your highest level of consciousness and alertness? More consciousness and alertness than normal. I feel that my awareness was omnipresent during the Goldenness. It expanded vastly as I neared The Great Presence of Light. I was aware of all that is, was, and ever shall be. Whereas in this body I am aware of my insufficient awareness, except as an under-current.

Please compare your vision during the experience to your everyday vision that you had immediately prior to the time of the experience. My vision was not as if with these eyes. The closest to describe it is in meditation. When I say 'see' it is not with physical eyes but with simple awareness.

Please compare your hearing during the experience to your everyday hearing that you had immediately prior to the time of the experience. Hearing is different from listening. It is not through the ears but through awareness. I was aware of all, simultaneously without the effort of eyes or ears.

Did you see or hear any earthly events that were occurring during a time that your consciousness/awareness was apart from your

physical/earthly body? Yes. I saw the nurses standing over my bio-
logical body. The older nurse reacted to my death by becoming all controlling and in-charge, while the younger nurse was crying and getting
very upset. I could feel their personalities and knew they were worried about getting into serious trouble. They were dropping things and
rushing about, pushing alarm buttons and doing CPR on the body. I
couldn't wait to leave this place. When I awoke 2 days later, the young
nurse came to see me and told me that I had died for 6 minutes and
had been given more than 6 pints of blood. My arms and hands were
a mass of bruises where they had tried to stick their IV lines in.

What emotions did you feel during the experience? I felt profound
love, profound compassion, and incredible unity. I still feel all of it. Living in this world is like I have to 'pretend' to be someone I am not for
fear of recrimination and distrust. I pretend to be a happy-go-lucky
type who couldn't even spell the word 'profound'.

Did you pass into or through a tunnel? No.

Did you see an unearthly light? Yes. I saw and became one with the
pure Golden Light of the vast and great all-knowing wisdom of all that
is. Perhaps this is Nirvana; it certainly was bliss. All was alive with the
Goldenness; yet, it was all there ever could be. It was eternally perfect
and undisturbed. Once the clearer and even brighter light appeared,
I knew that was my ultimate goal – to reunite with my real and true
home, the source, holy essence, divine sweetness, nectar, and Divine
hearth. It could be no less than the supreme heart of all creation, beyond anything I have ever found described in any 'holy' book. I am
lost for words.

**Did you seem to encounter a mystical being or presence, or hear
an unidentifiable voice?** I encountered a definite being, or a voice
clearly of mystical or unearthly origin I felt the presence of a Being of
great power. His voice was pure and clear, but even that doesn't describe it. He was and is of Angelic potency. After my experience, I had
an actual meeting with him in broad daylight outside my house. I have
heard him call me in the night and he also guides me in life. This is
very difficult for me telling you but I feel it is my time to help, if I can
in some small way.

Did you encounter or become aware of any deceased (or alive) beings? Uncertain. This is difficult to explain. All of life is held in the Goldenness. It was in me, I in it, and I felt all. I was omnipresent. Therefore, I was connected to all creation, which includes everyone! But nobody was there right in front of me, yet everyone was there in the love! So I was aware of all "beings" from all states of being.

Did you become aware of past events in your life during your experience? Yes. I re-experienced every moment of my life in refined detail including all feelings, thoughts, sounds, smells, people, loves, hates, anger, sorrow, fear, happiness, fun times, food, and everything up until I was in the Goldenness. It was as if I had again lived my life, but from the standpoint of a witness.

Did you seem to enter some other, unearthly world? A clearly mystical or unearthly realm - I entered a Golden Light, which seemed to be that which contains all that is was and ever shall be. It is an omnipresent state of all knowing, all seeing, and sublime being. The light held me, supported me, and caressed me with pure Divinity. I gazed into it seeing each particle bouncing around like billions of teeny atoms sparkling all about and within me; for as far as I could see which was forever. Then in the distance the brilliance of the Great Presence appeared, causing me to fly in desperation towards it. This was my true home.

Did time seem to speed up or slow down? Everything seemed to be happening at once; or time stopped or lost all meaning. No time, only universe.

Did you suddenly seem to understand everything? Everything about the universe. I understood EVERYTHING! It was a wondrous feeling of knowing at a level beyond 'normal' feeling or knowing. Perhaps 'boundless wisdom' could describe it.

I knew how everything came about. I understood the causation of desire and addiction behaviors, yearning and fearful thoughts, materialistic grabbing, and how humans longed to find a way through these issues but give up due to constantly being magnetized to their fearful connections. They do not trust their own heartfelt truths, giving their energy to negative forces.

I knew everything about the world – its animals, insects, ocean life, plants and trees, water, air, fire, the winds, the sky, and song. All these things have life. I knew that The Great Mother Earth loves us all. There is harmony, which awaits silently in the background of all experience for those with eyes to see.

Reality is in the words Reality, Real Light, simultaneous experience, constancy, now-ness, a harmony beyond music, and purity of creation. I was experiencing being in the knowing of everything. I was aware of all and everything that is was and ever shall be. It was a feeling of great wonder, like a child of innocence yet ancient and fully comprehensible.

Did you reach a boundary or limiting physical structure? No.

Did you come to a border or point of no return? I came to a barrier that I was not permitted to cross; or was "sent back" against my will.

Did scenes from the future come to you? Scenes from the world's future. I saw how the world of people wanted to wake up, yet there were some people in places of power who would do all they could to stop it. Yet, I saw that some beings on Earth had such high awareness that they would create a chain reaction and start the event of awakening. This plan has been in 'the works' for many eons and is the natural outcome of what has been and why we are here. I saw that all is perfect, although it doesn't appear to be. This process of awakening will make the future assembly of humanity sing the one song. This is their true birthright and inheritance from the first Mother and Father who art in Heaven. I have seen a lot, but life is full of joy. Ultimately, we are as one verse.

We ascend into our light bodies, which look like holograms of light and color. To achieve the consciousness of the rainbow body is slightly different to the body of clear light. That is the personal future of beings.

As for the planet, there is a lot of work to do and we have to do it. It's as if Yin and Yang have a major argument. Then when they reach such an unbearable state, they will dissolve into each other and a completely new universe is born. At this stage, it is all like kids slugging it out in the backyard. Human beings are so immature at this stage; they have to keep fighting. On the positive side, there are many here now who understand, live a better way, and set a higher example and vibration for others. All those who have opened their hearts and minds to the new understandings have dropped fearful thought forms. They are now free to live lighter and happier lives. There are many earthquakes, rising oceans, and 600mph winds on the way. We do not need fear, for it is all known and meant to be.

Did you have a sense of knowing special knowledge or purpose?
Uncertain. I did feel I had a mission. My mission at the time was to get to the Great Presence, the most brilliant, clear light of the whole experience. That is every single being's mission in this universe. We are all together in our ultimate destination. We will all know joy beyond descriptive language.

Discuss any changes that might have occurred in your life after your experience: Large changes in my life. I have been to Heaven and Hell. Now, I am just Being here. It has been a long and difficult journey but I have enjoyed finding a few pearls of wisdom. I am now beginning to relax into my real self as I mature, but this is a slow process. I hope I can achieve some good before I depart. I wish to allow myself the luxury of becoming an 'authentic' human being for the benefit of all sentient beings.

Did you have any changes in your values or beliefs after the experience that occurred as a result of the experience? Yes. I didn't want to be here on earth anymore. I was suicidal until my forties, but always knew the work had to be done whilst in the body. I felt that everyone was just living a lie and I was frustrated that I couldn't do anything about it. I felt so alone. I tried to tell people to get into the light of joy but they wouldn't take me seriously, so I gave up. Honestly, it's taking me a lifetime to figure out how to live here. I had to learn to hide my true thoughts everywhere I go. Nowadays, being older and a bit wiser, I just laugh at myself and don't worry so much.

Do you have any psychic, non-ordinary or other special gifts after your experience that you did not have before the experience? Yes. I can attune to certain Beings of wisdom. I can understand people at a deep level. I see visions. Sometimes I see people who have just died. They come to me afraid of their next step. I do I Ching readings and sometimes I do healing massage. I have had experiences with extra-terrestrials of incredible loving kindness. It is difficult to write all this stuff here.

Have you ever shared this experience with others? Yes. I had never spoken of this to anyone except a counselor who said nothing; being as she could not in her capacity as a counselor, share her feelings. I felt very alone and could not find the validation of the experience that I was seeking.

Last year I shared my experience with a friend called Geoff, at his house in France. This year he sent me a book, saying, "This is you Yaz.... *Dying to be Me* by Anita Moojani." This made me cry tears of joy that another one has seen with similar eyes. Your email address is in the book, so that is how I came to the website to find many others like myself.

Did you have any knowledge of near death experience (NDE) prior to your experience? No.

What did you believe about the reality of your experience shortly (days to weeks) after it happened? Experience was definitely real. I knew that I had the most amazing experience of my life.

What do you believe about the reality of your experience at the current time? Experience was definitely real. Yes it was and still is real. I see things differently than others most of the time. I feel that I can't speak my truth because people have such strong opinions about everything. I cannot be bothered to enter into any arguments about ultimate reality.

Have your relationships changed specifically as a result of your experience? Yes. I have always struggled with relationships, but people seem to love having me around. I worry they may become unhappy with me if I get too honest.

Have your religious beliefs/spiritual practices changed specifically as a result of your experience? Yes. I have looked into many different spiritual paths, desperate to find something like me. Tibetan Buddhism came close. I receive many messages from beyond this realm and I used to write it all down. This is constant, getting the messages are from 'above.' Some of it seems imperative but where would one express such sentences? I do not know.

At any time in your life, has anything ever reproduced any part of the experience? Yes. I have moments when reality transforms before my eyes. Although this sounds impossible, everything becomes the hologram. It is full of color and living light. The whole world is not as it at first appears. I guess once one has seen the world in true light, it just happens automatically thereafter.

Did the questions asked and information that you provided accurately and comprehensively describe your experience? Yes. I feel that I have been as open as I can at this time, considering I have had a lot of 'messages ' coming through as I write. The sense of excitement is great around me now, yet there is a certain peace here too. I do hope that I have made it easy for you to read and that it does make for some inspiration.

Are there one or several parts of your experience that are especially meaningful or significant to you? The whole experience has been with me every day since it happened 35 years ago. Many meaningful synchronicities have happened since that time.

Is there anything else that you would like to add about your experience? I feel I was touched by a Holiness or Sacredness of spirit. It runs through me at certain times, particularly when a person near me is needing assistance, it fills me up and pours through me into them although they are unaware of it they like to have me around. At the same time, I can be quite drained if stay too long with a person who is closed, which most are, in my experience. I wish everyone could see what I see and be uplifted.

TEN

Lisa had three NDEs, starting at age 10. There is no universally accepted definition for the NDE. When NDERF reviews them, if a person faints and loses consciousness, it is considered an imminently life-threatening event. So, it does qualify as a NDE. Lisa had called her experiences a "Life and Death Experiences" (LDE). I changed the reference to NDE in the story below so it would be consistent with the rest of the book and also so it didn't confuse readers.

Lisa's description of what it is like to merge with God is wonderful!

LISA T.

It was a beautiful day and I was feeling good. Then without warning, I felt an eerie sensation that scared me. I cried out to Jesus to save me. When my head hit the floor, I felt an intense pain in my head.

Suddenly, my spirit left the body and floated up into the rafters of the old farmhouse. Then I was in another place being lovingly embraced into this beautiful golden amber light. It was like a golden, amber colored bubble of pure love. There was no pain. I felt only joy, peace, happiness, and contentment. I had no thoughts of what had taken place. I became one with the Light, totally and completely. I was totally embraced in the arms of the living God. I felt totally protected and loved. Every thought was telepathic. There are really no words to express the intense and complete love I felt since it is beyond anything I had ever experienced. I had never felt such an intense love.

Then as a leaf falls from a tree, I began to look down and when I did, my spirit began to re-enter my body. I was never told that I would be coming back, but like the event itself, it was done so without warning. There was no one around; it was as though the Lord breathed Life back into me.

When I came to after my first experience, I was sad that I was back here on earth. I struggled with that. The difficult part was not having anyone who was another 10 year old to share this with. I tried my best to understand what took place, but I had no one to share my story with. This amazing experience would become my sacred secret. I was afraid that if I shared my story with others that I would be called "Crazy," so I remained quiet and told nobody.

In 1982, I was 19 years old at the time of my second experience too place. I had moved to California hoping for a new beginning in the next chapter of my life. On a hot summer day, some family and friends decided to go behind one of the homes where there was a river. The river was cold and deep. I never learned to swim. I knew that several of my friends had been lifeguards. Since they reassured me they would be nearby if I needed any help, I jumped into the ffeezing waters. I swallowed water, but managed to get to the surface of the river twice.

On my third attempt to stop myself drowning, I saw an old movie screen of my life being played out. It started from the day of my birth up to the day of what would be my funeral. As I watched my family crying, I cried out, "No. No!" Instantly, I was lifted out of the water and brought to the shore. Everyone was quite concerned. I never told anyone what I had seen. They told me that since I jumped into the current, I was down the river a ways so they had to go some distance before they could get to me.

The third experience took place in Florida. I was now a wife and a mother. I was going to having an angiogram test. I was very concerned about the test because my dad had died from an angiogram test many years earlier. I asked the doctors if there was any other test that could be done to isolate the problem. They said that I needed the angiogram.

The day of the test was one that filled me with anxiety. People and doctors were constantly reassuring me that I would be fine and reminding me that they do this procedure all the time at the heart center I was going to. As the procedure began, I moaned with discomfort. I was praying, then suddenly, everything went pitch black. I felt no pain and was wondering what was happening. Then I heard the voices in the surgical unit.

My spirit was being lifted higher and higher until it popped out of my body and went up to the ceiling. I could see the room filled with doctors and nurses. The gown was torn off my body. Another female nurse came quickly to the side of the bed with a large bowl of iodine and a sponge. She began to start rubbing my chest down while another large man was now on top of my body with his hands hitting my chest. He began pressing down on my chest. None of it hurt me. I was amused by everything that I was seeing. As I was watching, I realized that they were about to cut open my chest. I thought, "Wow, recovery is really gonna hurt."

Next, I heard a voice repeating, "Lisa, open your eyes!" I finally opened my eyes. Later, I was told by the medical staff that I went into V-tach and coded on the table. The procedure that was supposed to take an hour, actually took several hours.

To this day, I still struggle in sharing all three of my stories to a degree, because unless one goes through it, it is difficult to express the depths of love one receives. The other two NDEs made me aware of the fact that Life and Death are more than Precious. Death can come without ANY warning, and that we need to be ready at any time. It has also helped me in the grieving process when I lost my dad, other members of family, or friends that I have loved. It is a reassurance that there is so much more waiting for them.

In the 41 years since I had my first experience, I have strongly felt that love is the greatest gift that we can give and receive from one another.

At the time of your experience was there an associated life-threatening event? Uncertain. At the age of ten I had no previous diagnosis of any medical condition.

Was the experience difficult to express in words? Uncertain. Because I have had three different NDEs, it is harder to express how they have all varied. But the last NDE was hard to come back. Twice it is Difficult to come back, but the third time it was HARD to come back. Going through the NDE three times, I felt very alone, very puzzled as to WHY I was STILL here. I recalled asking in prayer, Wasn't I good enough? Of course, I have come to realize that I have more work to do, SHARING My Stories is part of it. To give HOPE to those who do not understand or believe that there is Life after Death. To encourage others.

At what time during the experience were you at your highest level of consciousness and alertness? More consciousness and alertness than normal immediately AFTER I left my body. This life is like living in a world that is Black and White, verses when my heart stopped and I was in the Spiritual realm, where everything is so much more vivid, alive, beautiful, and pure. When I came back, it's like the NDE is the clearest moment one endures; I can recall ALL of it. Unlike daily life, it is difficult to explain how ALIVE I was when I was "dead." But in truth, I was MORE ALIVE THEN than what I am here and now. The emotions, feelings, sound, and smells - everything is much more INTENSE, it is ALIVE!

Please compare your vision during the experience to your everyday vision that you had immediately prior to the time of the experience. Everyday life is like living in light pastel colors, while if we were to take a look at a color wheel, we would see EVERY Color and then MORE. Like waking up on a cloudy gloomy day, compared to a Bright Sunny Day.

Please compare your hearing during the experience to your everyday hearing that you had immediately prior to the time of the experience. Hearing during these events was very intense, NOT Loud but CLEARER. In the everyday arena, it's like I have to repeat what was said. Not during a NDE. It is 100% clear without any questions.

Did you see or hear any earthly events that were occurring during a time that your consciousness/awareness was apart from your physical/earthly body? Yes. During my first NDE, I was totally One with this Brilliant Light of Love. This Light I felt was God the Father Almighty, being embraced into Him, I became One with Him. I had no need to speak, because everyone knows the thoughts. When I came back, it was difficult to express myself. I had other things that began to take place afterwards heavenly dreams, as well as open visions, where I would be on One place spiritually but somewhere else physically.

What emotions did you feel during the experience? I felt Love, Pure Love, happiness, joy, peace, and contentment.

Did you pass into or through a tunnel? Uncertain. If I went through a tunnel, I would not have described it as such. Everything was instantly bright so I didn't see a tunnel. I was instantly with the Father.

Did you see an unearthly light? Yes. A Beautiful Brilliant Golden/ Amber light. The color also reflected the Intensity of the pure Love I was embraced in. I have never seen such a color here on earth.

Did you seem to encounter a mystical being or presence, or hear an unidentifiable voice? I encountered a definite being, or a voice clearly of mystical or unearthly origin. This Brilliant Golden/Amber Light was ALIVE, I was embraced into this Light which held me deeply. I became One with the Light. It was Pure Love, just Glorious!

Did you encounter or become aware of any deceased (or alive) beings? No.

Did you become aware of past events in your life during your experience? Yes. I had a very FAST Life Review during my Drowning NDE, but to recall everything I had seen would be nearly impossible to mention it all. I recognized my Birth and what would have been my funeral if I had chosen to go that day.

Did you seem to enter some other, unearthly world? Some unfamiliar and strange place. It was definitely not earth, but to say it was mystical or strange would be incorrect. To me, it felt like a place I had known and I was very much at peace with that.

Did time seem to speed up or slow down? Everything seemed to be happening at once - or time stopped or lost all meaning. There was absolutely no TIME. It was as if time stood still.

Did you suddenly seem to understand everything? Everything about myself and others. I became more aware of other things, in which prior I did not have much interest, I was now more captivated. I felt in Harmony, but it was NOT of this World, NOR did it really have anything to do with any form of conflict to nature.

Did you reach a boundary or limiting physical structure? Uncertain. I now occasionally have dreams or visions which are very real, bringing me to other locations, spiritually, as an Open Vision. When I first had my first NDE, I COULD Sense when the phone would ring, etc.

Did you come to a border or point of no return? No. All three of my NDEs were Sudden and that seemed to be the way I returned back to my body as well.

Did scenes from the future come to you? Scenes from the world's future. In the Dream State, and some of those things have taken place.

Did you have a sense of knowing special knowledge or purpose? Yes. That I was to Love as He Loved me. When I was embraced into Him, it was with all my faults and errors, HE STILL LOVED ME.

Discuss any changes that might have occurred in your life after your experience. Large changes in my life. I do feel that my dreams are often forms of communication the Lord is having with me, whether it is about a warning, or things to come, or embracing me to give me strength.

Did you have any changes in your values or beliefs after the experience that occurred as a result of the experience? Yes. Because I was only ten years old during my first NDE, I would say that my Life changed early on. I realize that there is a Higher Authority and that Life can be taken quickly.

Do you have any psychic, non-ordinary or other special gifts after your experience that you did not have before the experience? Uncertain. Every once in a while, I can sense when something isn't right, or will have a dream that comes to pass. This I do not recall having prior to the experience.

Have you ever shared this experience with others? Yes. It is now in a Book. *My Sacred Secrets, My journeys through Life and Death*. I have also shared my experience with family and friends.

Did you have any knowledge of near death experience (NDE) prior to your experience? No.

What did you believe about the reality of your experience shortly (days to weeks) after it happened? Experience was definitely real. Just felt I had gone through the most Powerful thing, and not able to share it with another living soul, was extremely difficult. I had suffered a cracked skull from the fall, and most likely recovering from those symptoms.

What do you believe about the reality of your experience at the current time? Experience was definitely real. There was no doubt I had been in the arms of the Lord, what I saw and felt I still feel today.

Have your relationships changed specifically as a result of your experience? Yes. More understanding and compassionate.

Have your religious beliefs/spiritual practices changed specifically as a result of your experience? Yes. I wish to be more pleasing before the Lord and do more for others.

At any time in your life, has anything ever reproduced any part of the experience? No.

Did the questions asked and information that you provided accurately and comprehensively describe your experience? Yes.

Are there one or several parts of your experience that are especially meaningful or significant to you? The INTENSE Love I felt during the first NDE and the angst feeling of "WHY AM I STILL HERE?" after the Third. It is extremely difficult going through these events and walking in a world that is truly Black and White, where there is such violence and hate, compared to the Love and Joy, which I experienced.

ELEVEN

I hinted earlier that there was one person I knew who had a hellish NDE as a test of spirit. His experience was like the ancient alchemy idea of walking through the fire of purification. I get chills when I think of how insidious hell is. Normally, you think of hell as being fire and brimstone. But in Cougar's experience, evil people started with half-truths about how they were the truth of God. Then when that didn't work, they tried to tempt him with all manner of earthly delights. Then when that failed, they used fear and force. This process is how evil works, even on earth.

The other interesting part of Cougar's experience is that it is similar to the ancient Sumerian story of Innana. This begs the question whether the experience was a ritual right of passage of the human spirit; known to the ancient people of Sumeria. Or perhaps, it could be a culmination of reincarnation. No matter though, this is an amazing experience that I consider in my top 5 NDEs I have ever read.

COUGAR

I have had one surface experience and two deep ones. I have been to heaven and to hell and personally resolved the apparent dichotomy of experiences. My first experience was at age 11.

The wind was knocked out of me from a high swing set fall. My diaphragm was in shock. I couldn't move. What a terrifying moment! I couldn't breathe in. I could only breathe out, so I kept what little air I had in me. I was going to die. I finally accepted it and relaxed. I said goodbye to it all. I could feel the entire earth behind me. I could only move my eyes. Everything became more alive. The leaves on the trees grew greener. The blue of the sky grew bluer. I have never seen such beauty in nature before! Then I saw the past come up out of the ground; the last 400 years anyway. I became the nose of an old Native American. I could easily distinguish each type of tree by its smell alone. When strangers came to this land to claim it for their own I gained a new perspective of the Native Americans vs. the English. Also, it used to be fun to play soldier, but after seeing what I saw from the civil war, I gained a new respect for human life. (I didn't realize until much later that this experience happened to me on the 100th anniversary of the beginning of the civil war only 126 miles away).

I was released from the earth and floated through different layers of the atmosphere. I felt a mature love surround me; a love beyond what I have experienced from my parents or even from my grandparents. A voice filled my head and said everything was o.k. I surrendered to it. I was going home! Suddenly, there was an explosion of air shoved down my throat. I was back in my body. Delicious aromatic air filled my lungs, rejuvenating me.

My second NDE was a deep one happening at age 24 in 1974, while living in Colorado. I was given 3 prophetic warning dreams of a near future traffic accident. Why, I don't know. I was powerless to stop it. It was a head on collision. I was flung into the air, away from my motorcycle and out of my body. I saw my body crumple to the ground. My back was broken in two places.

A cool gray fog enveloped me and swirled into a tunnel of light, taking me upward into the heavens. I felt this increasing love come to me and at the same time a faint sound growing stronger and stronger, swelling up and surrounding me into a rich full "HUU." The hum was also centered inside me. A voice came forth from within the sound. This was like the drone of a thousand prop-driven airplanes or extended rolling thunder. This voice felt like a great grandfather's voice that loved me like a son. It knew everything about me and spoke it to me. Even my shortcomings were mentioned in love and understanding.

Meanwhile, I was being taken over enormous pastoral landscapes and up into a huge alabaster temple at the top of a mountain. The "HUU" permeated from everywhere inside. There were vast archways and pillars reaching up into a high vaulted dome. These seemed to be made of thick alabaster-type rock. They glowed from the inside out. I was led into one chamber that showed me things dealing with people who were asleep on earth yet learning here. I was led into the main chamber where I beheld a light shining from a lectern. In this light were seven beings of light connected to each other by the light. They were one, yet seven. The love leaping to me from these seven faces of God reminded me of the experience I had when I was eleven. It was familiar, and made me feel at home. The seven beings of light spoke of one accord, inside my head, for the voice did not travel from across the room. They filled my head with their wisdom. As they spoke, it was as if the chamber disappeared, for the pictures they put in my head seemed to fill the whole room like a giant picture screen, the only difference was, I was in the picture myself as if everything was alive around me.

I was being shown the future of mankind. It was not a peaceful future from the start. It was disturbing and almost too incredible to bear. I had been so naive and idealistic. Now this was taken away from me, my innocence. I saw individual starvation and famine. I saw wars and pain and selfish manipulation, and bodies lying strewn all over huge battlefields. "How can there be so much cruelty in the world?!" I thought and shook my head in dismay. I did not want to see this. Although there was a powerful fascination in seeing something like on such a large scale, there was no way I was going to participate in any of it. Then came a scene that was a crucial turning point form me. I saw a man in a cowboy hat riding furiously on the range along with cattle and other men with rifles. It was in black and white like some old cowboy movie. On this one man, my attention was drawn to the pale red letters "R.R." emblazoned on his chest. "Who is this?" I asked. I did not have to use my mouth to speak. The voice told me, "He will become the president of the United States." "Roy Rogers?" I couldn't help thinking to myself, "This isn't making any sense." So, I doubted my vision for many years.

The angels told me, "What you are looking at are the probable future events of your planet, but they don't have to happen if you are willing to change. Everything is in flux and can change when change is necessary individually and planetarily." I saw beyond the year 2000 and then I saw my own personal future; what I will be doing in the last moments of my life. Active, happy. I had mixed feelings and limited understanding of the meaning of this at the time.

A torrential roar like a waterfall passed through my head. The gray fog came back. Then my eyes opened straight away. There was no tunnel on the return trip. I saw the inside of an ambulance. Voices fading away in my head were promising of future visits to me.

Six years later, in 1980, Ronald Reagan was elected president of the United States; an actor turned president. This was the cowboy I saw in the future prophecy with the initials "R.R." emblazoned on his chest.

In 1994, I discovered "Near-Deather Dan" wrote about his experience of being taken into a cathedral and shown future prophecy also. He saw, in 1975, editorial cartoons of a cowboy actor, and the initials "R.R." under the presidential seal. This happened to him within a year of my NDE. Amazing! We saw the same thing near the same time. The only difference was "lightning boy" thought it was Robert Redford, I thought it was Roy Rogers. Incredible! We were both wrong, but we were both right also! This is what I call a significant coincidence. But wait! There is more! We were both born within a month of each other in the same year, and I have the dubious honor of graduating from the same high school and in the same class as Dan. Coincidence is a lazy word we use when we just don't see the bigger picture.

In 1987, while learning from Grandpa Roberts, an 84 year-old Cherokee elder living in California, I fell ill. Grandpa saw my fever as not only a physical illness but with his spiritual eye he saw it as an initiation. As he studied me, he became worried. He saw something powerful but said only, "many people die upon entering this place you are going, and the ones that survive are permanently mad." That didn't help much, but at least he told me the truth so I could brace myself. He said if I can't find love anywhere to at least leave the door open to love and he will be on the other side waiting. He directed me to go out to a sacred circle and survive it, alone. He was to do much needed ceremony himself from inside his pod house.

I was weak from alternating between one moment shaking from internal chills to sweating with heat. An owl called hauntingly. (Some natives consider the owl a bringer of life, others, a messenger of death.) The last time I passed out was 7 AM. Then, I woke up dead. Although this experience is written about somewhat more in my book, *Angels in the Light*, I refuse to document it here, again, to not give it any more power, except to say I woke up suspended in the pit of hell. I was a mortal caught between an immortal battle of good and evil. Evil was allowed the reins for a time to show me its nightmarish glory. The dark great grandmother and dark great grandfather came to me to show me their perverted version of creation and their history and purpose. I was their spawn, their chosen kindred. They wrapped their tentacles tightly around my cells and my soul. The Bible's protective charm does not work here: "Yea, though I walk through the valley of the shadow of death . . ." Ha! What a cruel joke! You are stripped totally naked there. No protection whatsoever. Nada. No sword, no shield, no logic, not one ounce of love down there to hold onto. Fear and despair rule the dark day. The only hope left I could find was to not fear to the point of death by decimation, for you will be filled with terrors to a degree unknown by most mortals.

Thanks be to the Eternals and Grandpa Roberts, I miraculously survived and regained my sanity. Only last week did I discover I had taken a journey of epic proportions, a universal myth. I had only a fragment of the Assyrian Descent of Ishtar from the 7th century B.C. Today, in September 2000, I have discovered a complete text of the Sumerian prototype called Inanna's Journey to Hell from before the 18th century B.C. A full 7 of the 8 elements of the story are exactly what happened to me. I witnessed it firsthand and furthermore, I can report the dialogue they were forbidden to report. I also have permission to report some of the dialogue of heaven, that which was previously forbidden by the words of Revelations 10:4, "And when the seven thunders had sounded, I was about to write, but I heard a voice from heaven saying, "Seal up what the Seven thunders have said, and do not write it down."

Needless to say, now I am on fire with what Kimberly Clark Sharp calls "Woo-Woos." Painfully, my mouth is shut to neighbors and friends. I crave to shout it out among the rooftops! Yet here I sit, quietly writing. Researchers ask about personal changes after NDEs. The gifts first:

I have timely documentation to show my IQ went from normal to superior and up. Of course, when one is given a life changing increase in perception and awareness, some of its fallout shows up in the area sometimes known as IQ. I was thinking more globally instead of selfish locally. I have an affinity for Cliff Robertson in Flowers for Algernon (Charly).

I was given patience and the ability to see behind people's conscious and unconscious masks. I was given the power to leave my body, the power to limited healing, to slow my heart rate, to reach the theta state. I was given more power to love, but still feel smaller than a candle being held out to the sun. You see, the all-encompassing love in the heavens defies description and has no match anywhere else.

The curses are the alienation it brings, especially at such a young age. The power to blow out light bulbs, several streetlights in a row, transformers, billboard lights, the power to stop an interviewer's tape recorder, the power to start broken battery operated toys. The power of not merely mind reading, but pure telepathy (as above with the beings of light, so below with us). What? You don't call that a curse? It may be whimsical to part clouds with a mere thought or to find that parking space you need open, to get a phone call from someone you are just now thinking of or to finish someone's sentences. It may feel wonderful to have a wild bird land on your outreaching arm, with no food in your hand, as you are saying goodbye to a week spent on Mt. Shasta."

I may have warm fuzzy memories of telepathically calling cats to come to me, known and unknown cats from other rooms and outdoors, most anytime I desired, but what of the occasional depressed dark days that you go out for a drive to clear your head and attract a big black dog to slam itself against the side of your moving vehicle so hard that it shakes the vehicle (accompanied with one threateningly deep "woof"), just because it senses you don't like dogs? (Later, a 20 year friend of the owner said that dog never does that).

It may aid in a relationship to feel the fear inside you from someone else's hidden fear so that it can be brought out into the light of day for discussion and possible release. But what of the time you are so upset, while simultaneously practicing verbal control consciously, that you telepathically shout at a loved one so intensely that later, when you are being readdressed on what you said to them, they get upset when you try to convince the person that you did not say it out loud? (She swore she heard it. I knew I did not say it aloud).

It is a busy street. 100 cars per minute pass a pedestrian in both directions. You are virtually indistinguishable being in one of those 100 cars per minute. Mere time spent walking on the sidewalk has desensitized her to the blur of cars going by. You are becoming attracted to her on your approach but don't want to call attention to yourself. To your surprise she is getting better looking the closer you get. You want to look away, but can't for long. Your vehicle isn't particularly loud or smelly but she still goes out of her way to turn around and look at you, straight in the eyes! As you pass her you look back in the rear view mirror for as long as you cannot to admire her any longer but to see if she looks at anyone else in traffic . . . She does not. What? This doesn't sound so bad a curse after all? Perhaps it is even a pleasant surefire attention getter. Perhaps you can even be recognized with parlor trick popularity? Let's go a little deeper then. To hear people thinking things totally different than they are saying? This level of telepathy has led people into madness. Some people want to harness it but to learn to turn it off and on at will, one loses it to a large degree. But to not harness it is to open up the higher, more dangerous levels: To have telepathic control over other people's bodies even to the point of succeeding against their will. Contrary to the comforting "writ in stone" hypnotists blather about, to make people do whatever you will them to do. To invite telepathy in, you may invite it all in, to a degree that people do not know of in this world today. To even kill telepathically! Most deny the possibility of any and all of this.

Can we handle such responsibility and power and not abuse it? I have discovered no benefits to telepathy in this world as it is today. People are not ready for it. In my opinion it can only be abused today. Telepathic violence cannot even be touched by the law. It is above the law. Furthermore, telepathic powers are debunked as utter nonsense that makes it even more delicious and tempting by the few who enter this place of power prematurely. It is free to be abused under the directions and limitations of only spiritual law, which exists invisibly to us.

So, perhaps it is time for me to tell you a story. The time feels ripe in the telling of it, to not take telepathy lightly or wistfully desiring it: When I was much younger, I heard directly from two people who claimed to have had this power to kill from a distance. The price they paid was huge. Divorce, loss of jobs, loss of health and many regrets. I didn't know what to think of the reality of this at the time. But I surely was not going to challenge them about it. Then, one day, I experienced being a witness to the probability of this power so strongly that it was a very sobering experience for me.

I know a man (I shall call him Paul) who twenty-six years ago was separated from his spouse and was heading toward divorce. One day he lost his cool in front of me in his house. Cursing his pain he fell into a trance. He could not be distracted from his task. He psychically located her new boyfriend (I shall call him Jon). Jon was about three blocks away in traffic. Paul threw his anger on Jon like a black cloud. Paul had felt that he lost his soul mate for this lifetime because of Jon's insidious inclusion into his wife's life while they were still together. Jon, using everything gathered from conversations with her about Paul claimed to be richer, stronger, more intelligent, and he introduced her to cocaine. He persisted with all his lies until she could no longer resist him. Knowing Jon did not play fair, it was a great relief to release this anger on him. Paul was finally at peace. Yet, only then, Paul realized that even such a crime against him should go unpunished by him... and an old spiritual law came into his head that it would come back on him threefold. Moments after discharging his hate toward him, Paul took the black blanket off from around him and brought it back into himself. But was it too late?

Over the years, Paul's wife had grown accustomed to uncanny events happening around him. When she left Jon at the hospital, she was at Paul's doorstep in a heartbeat. This was her first visit since the break-up. She strongly suspected that he had something to do with it since she knew he didn't like Jon and that it was such a freak accident. She confronted him with it and he admitted to it through his confusion of love and anguish. Jon was lucky he did not die but he was permanently injured with a compression fracture to his lower back. She also discovered that Paul could not walk for three days and was helpless enough that she would get his meals for him during that time. Paul only then realized the extent of what could have happened to Jon. There is much discussion left in this topic of telepathy before reaching true understanding, to reach wisdom. There is a sadness in wisdom. Oh, to be happy. To be innocent! But we can't go back.

The seven beings of light did what they prophesied. They came to me in the next three years after my 1974 NDE and took me onward. They came to me in dreams and between dreams pulling me into full conscious awareness. They came one at a time, each with a specific task. They took me through and above the world. They showed me the universe. They took me into the heavens and showed me some of the planes of existence as we all journey upward into the face of the "un-created creating." They took me into past lives. Whether they are my past lives or just "past lives", I can't say. But then, that doesn't matter to me. What does matter is that I learned a great deal from these lives as if I had lived them. My book, Angels in the Light details some of these past lives and heavenly realms. Its like Zardoz's "Out of Time Touch Teaching," learning years' worth of stuff in mere moments. So, effectively, I have lived all those lives, you see?

As an extra bonus given to me within the past life arena, I experienced a painful mortal death. In this way, I felt my own immortality upon my return. That physical death does not end life. This only supports the NDE feeling of immortality. It has gone beyond belief into experience, and thus we come to know for sure, first hand. This is a fount for much wisdom.

Once, from one angel, I was give the second ten of the now twenty commandments, with one important difference; the first ten are "thou shalt nots" the second ten are "thou shalts." These cannot be understood very well until one has passed through the lessons of the first ten, the foundation. This is not biblical. This is spiritual. I was also taken to visit other people who were once famous by earthly standards so I could see their progression in the worlds to come. The reason was so I could measure that from the basis of familiarity of who they once were. This also lent support to knowing human immortality by seeing others live on and continuing in their personal growth. Just because we die, doesn't mean that it is all over or that we can now just kick back and reap the rewards of the afterlife. There is much more work and responsibility to take on, but, yes, much more fairness and fun too!!

These angels taught me that we are all connected, that all of life is precious, that finding love within us is hard work, that we must generate more love more often, for human love pales before Eternal love. I am smaller than a candle being held out to the sun.

Spirit Love, Cougar

COUGAR-INANNA PARALLELS

"My third NDE was caused by fever and I think, borderline coma. This was a journey into the Pit. 13 years later, I discover that my journey into Hell was strangely similar to an ancient myth before the 18th century BC. My journey into Hell was astoundingly similar to that of Inanna's journey. Here are the twenty similar items within our stories:

1.) Inanna looking into the abyss from the summits of Heaven. I was looking into the abyss from the sacred medicine wheel circle.
2.) Inanna held curiosity in her life. I hold a quest for all truth.
3.) Prayer to Heaven by a minister for her sake. Prayer to Heaven by a medicine man for my sake.
4.) The holy men beat a drum for our sakes.
5.) The holy ritual was done after we had already left for Hell.
6.) We both entered Hell wearing our Immortality.
7.) We both had a golden ring grasped in our hands.
8.) Similar statements: A land from which no traveler returns/very few people survive this journey.
9.) Both are stripped naked.
10.) Surprising LAW of the underworld to be stripped naked.

11.) Ereshkigal, Great Queen of the Dark World. In my NDE, the appearance of the Dark Great grandmother and Dark Great grandfather.

12.) Inanna dropped on her knees/I passed out while saying respectfully, "Thank you but no thanks." when offered this dark form of immortality.

13.) 7 Judges pronounced sentence on Inanna. Seven Judges from my Heavenly experience would not come to my rescue.

14.)   They spoke the sentence of the accursed to Inanna. They showed me their version of creation and their history.

15.) Both of us were sickened to death by the hellish stories.

16.) Her body hung on a spike. My body was suspended above the Pit on a cold, steel bridge that was two feet wide.

17.) We both returned from the dead, from a place from which no one returns.

18.) Two beings created by Enki to buzz the gate of Hell like flies. Two bees at my eye level seeing my return from the Pit at the sacred circle.

19.) The two rescuing beings were not to eat or drink in Hell. I used similar wisdom to resist seduction in Hell.

20.) We both came back with demons clinging to us."

TWELVE

Jean's experience is very inspirational. The life review and unconditional love are responsible for the most changes in behavior when she came back to earth. Here, Jean had a life review; but the most important thing to her was to remain worthy of the unconditional love she had experienced on the other side. She talks of the lessons we learn on earth and how the major events in our lives are there to gauge our progress in learning about love. Jean asked about the true religion. Her answer was that there is no one-size-fits-all religion. Each religion has certain lessons we learn on our path to God. The most important lessons we learn on earth are about love through our human relationships and caring for each other.

JEAN R.

I woke up lying in my hospital bed, but unable to breathe. Every joint in my body was in excruciating pain. I was panicky. I felt that if only my clothes were off, maybe my skin could breathe for me. I knew I was in trouble. I couldn't find the button to call a nurse. I thought, "I am just a bother and they hid the buzzer for the nurse. They want me to die." My panic rose and my thoughts were irrational. I had to talk myself down from this and apply some logic. I told myself, "I am in a hospital. They have put the call button somewhere and probably close. Stay calm and look." I found it at my upper right, wound around the bed rail. I remember such pain as I finally found the button and pushed it. The nurse answered and asked what I needed. I told her I felt panic and could not breathe.

She came to my room and talked to me soothingly, while she took my blood pressure. It was 0/30 and thus, my long journey through near death began.

In the days that followed, my heart stopped beating 4 times and my family was told that I most likely would not make it. This time for me is blurry and I had two near death experiences, but do not know which times they happened.

The first time, I went through a light (it is the only way I can describe this) and I was totally saturated in unconditional love. It was the most wonderful experience I have ever had. Unconditional love saturated me and it was so filling!

I then went through a life review. It was all about my relationships with others in this review. During this, I felt what they felt in my relationship with them. I felt their love or their pain or their hurt, by things I had done or said to them. Their hurt or pain made me cringe and I found myself thinking, "Oooh, I could have done better there." But most of what I felt was love, so it was not too bad. No one was judging me during this process. I felt no disapproval from anyone else, only my own reactions to it all. That feeling of unconditional love saturating me continued to be there. I was judging myself, but no one else was judging me in this review.

I was then asked if I wanted to come home (meaning there) or wanted to come back here. I told them that my two sons needed me and I had to go back. I was suddenly in my body again, feeling my achy joints flaring in pain. But I really don't remember what was going on around me at that point...just that I hurt. I still felt that love though and could rest.

The second experience, I found myself in a city and was told that this was the City of God. I was at a water fountain with a man in a long white linen robe tied around the waist with a chord. He told me I could ask any question I wanted and said he would take me on a tour. Because I had been raised at a time where Catholics said to even go into another Christian church was a mortal sin, and Lutherans said that those Catholics were going to go Hell, because they had statuary in their churches and prayed to saints, I had a very pressing question. The first question I asked was, "What is the right religion?"

I was told, "They all are. Each religion is a pathway trying to reach the same place." I was shown a mountain, with each religious group trying to reach the top, separated from each other by distance, but each one was trying to get to the same place.

I was then told that people choose to be born into whichever religion or group that will help them achieve the lessons they are sent here to learn. I was told the earth is like a big school; a place where you can apply spiritual lessons learned and test yourself, under pressure, to see if you can actually "live" the way you already know you should. The earth is a place to walk the walk and literally live the way it should be done. It was made clear to me that some people come to the earth to work on only one aspect of themselves, while others come to work on several aspects. Then there are others who come to not only work on their own nature, but also to help the world as a whole.

The other side does not have the physical pressures that having a body has. Here on earth, you must feed and clothe that body and provide shelter for it from the elements. You are under continual pressure of some sort, to make decisions that have a spiritual base. You are taught on the "other side" what you are "supposed to do," but can you LIVE it under these pressures on earth? From what I saw and heard there—on the others side, it is all about relationships and taking care of each other. Perfection is not expected of people, but learning is expected and considered good progress.

All of our experiences in a lifetime tend to follow some sort of pattern and often will recreate the same lessons, only in a different way, and under various circumstances. This is how you know what you are here to learn and test. If you examine the patterns, certain themes will become clear.

I was shown a library filled with gold covered books. These are the lives of people on earth where their life plan is laid out and what they hope to achieve through certain key experiences. From what I was shown, people have free choice as to how to get to these preset key experiences. They can take a meandering path of experiences or a more direct route, but there are certain events that are preset and will happen, no matter what. Each of those key events are benchmarks and one's reactions to them will show how much they have learned and what more needs to be done, or learned.

The economic turmoil we are now going through is one of those "world events" that was preset. People have a choice as to how to react to these events. From what I was shown, the spiritual way is to help each other and help those in need. This is the ultimate act of love. But there is also the choice of becoming more protective and self centered, less sharing and keeping one's own possessions as primary in one's re-actions to what is there. This is a materialistic way of viewing it all...as if the material world is more than the connection between all of mankind. So what choices will the majority make? It is still to be seen. I was shown in 1981 that this time would come and that banks were paper empires, built on paper and nothing more. But, too, so are many other businesses, paper empires built to collapse under pressure. How do people react to all of this? This is the key event and will test many. Will they reach out and take care of each other, or will they become more and more self-centered and protective of the material? There are always choices in this, just to determine which choices individuals will make.

I was shown other parts of the city as well, where souls were working with people on earth—scientists, the arts, and more. There is always a push there to "inspire" those on earth to create beneficial things for humanity in every area.

There was so much more too. But, more than anything this place was filled with love, love of mankind, love of everyone on earth, and of the earth itself. Communications were transparent there, thoughts shared as in a conversation here. The people I saw were all working happily and in great joy.

Though I was also shown a much darker place too, where people did not seem to know that they had moved out of their bodies and continually fought each other for material things. Material possessions were their focus and all the actions were self-based there. But above them were also a legion of beings waiting. Whenever someone looked up and asked God for help they were whisked away to another place, a place more peaceful and tuned to God and God's love. But many seemed lost in this place, never looking up and never asking for help.

This city had many different places, all geared to a different need. There was a place of rest where souls could recover from traumatic lives on earth. There were working places where souls could help humankind and others grow and be more. There were libraries and theaters and schools. And there was also the Temple of God.

I was taken into this large hall and before me were beings of pure light. One was sitting directly in front of me on a chair or throne. These beings did not have human shape but were more like pure energy of light. I found myself prostrating before them in awe. The love that emanated from them, particularly the one in the center, was overwhelming. I definitely did not feel their equal, but did feel this great, great honor to be there. I was embraced by this entity in the center and told, "You have done well, My Child, and I am pleased." The love that came flowing through me and the approval made me weep.

Was this God? Was this the ultimate? I really don't know. I just know that I was and am so much less than this being and those who were nearby. Yet, the love was so wondrous to have too. I found myself, upon returning, wanting to just be worthy of that love.

What were the end results of these experiences? What did I take away from it?

I live my life in the moment, enthralled and appreciative of all the experiences. I love living this life.

I try to always "walk the walk" not just saying the right thing, but living it as much as possible.

I do not fear death. Though I am not anxious to leave this life. I still have much to do but death is not something I fear. I know I will someday go "home," and it is there, not here.

What is most important?

I would say it is human relationships, loving and caring for each other. Religion has its place and is there as a pathway to more, but it is not the ultimate in any way. Religions are not God - just pathways.

But emphasis should be on that golden rule; Love your neighbor as yourself. Take care of each other whenever you can.

At the time of your experience was there an associated life-threatening event? Yes. I had Toxic Shock Syndrome and my heart had stopped beating on four different occasions

Was the experience difficult to express in words? Yes. Any references used here to explain it has to be done in earthly and material terms, when the experience there was so much more. For example, to speak of going through a light and feeling saturated with unconditional love, is not doing it real justice. This light is not easily explained in material terms, though the description of light is the closest you can come to it.

At what time during the experience were you at your highest level of consciousness and alertness? I feel the entire experiences were at that level.

How did your highest level of consciousness and alertness during the experience compare to your normal everyday consciousness and

alertness? More consciousness and alertness than normal. As much as anything it was the ease of communication and how effortlessly you could change locations. Nothing was impossible.

Please compare your vision during the experience to your every-day vision that you had immediately prior to the time of the experience. It was more a sense of complete security and safety, and difficult to describe visually. The buildings in the city looked like milk glass to some degree with veins of gold going through it. But there seemed to be a great deal of flexibility to its construction as well. Seats seemed to be able to mold to your shape.

Please compare your hearing during the experience to your every-day hearing that you had immediately prior to the time of the experience. Thought transfer, rather than words.

Did you see or hear any earthly events that were occurring during a time that your consciousness/awareness was apart from your physical/earthly body? No.

What emotions did you feel during the experience? Love and clarity.

Did you pass into or through a tunnel? No.

Did you see an unearthly light? Yes. Both the light I went through and the light of the beings in the Temple were unearthly.

Did you seem to encounter a mystical being or presence, or hear an unidentifiable voice? I encountered a definite being, or a voice clearly of mystical or unearthly origin. As described earlier beings that seemed to be the energy of light, separate but without real form.

Did you encounter or become aware of any beings who previously lived on earth who are described by name in religions (for example: Jesus, Muhammad, Buddha, etc.)? Uncertain Again, those beings of light.

But, too, the beings above the darker place may be described more as "angels" I suppose. But, sometimes, they also shed tears as they waited for these souls to ask for help. Those drops would fall on those below too, but did not seem to be noticed.

Did you encounter or become aware of any deceased (or alive) beings? Yes. I saw some family members, but did not speak to them. They were busy in different places. However, I did not see everyone I know who has died, by any means.

Did you become aware of past events in your life during your experience? Yes. It was in the life review, but all from the perspective of the other people in my relationships and how they felt towards me during certain events or times

Did you seem to enter some other, unearthly world? A clearly mystical or unearthly realm.
I described this above.

Did time seem to speed up or slow down? Everything seemed to be happening at once; or time stopped or lost all meaning. Time did not really have any meaning. There was no sense of rush or delay either.

Did you suddenly seem to understand everything? Everything about the universe.
I could see purpose in everything and patterns became clear.

Did you reach a boundary or limiting physical structure? Uncertain.
There were sections to the city, but not really a sense of boundary. I did not want to get too close to the darker place though. I had the sensation that I did not want to get sucked into that place.

Did you come to a border or point of no return? I came to a definite conscious decision to "return" to life. I knew my children needed me.

Did scenes from the future come to you? Scenes from the world's future. There were several scenes from the world's future, including the economic turmoil we are going through now. Paper empires crumbling everywhere and people begging for mercy who deserved it not.

During your experience, did you encounter any specific information/awareness suggesting that there either is (or is not) continued existence after earthly life ("life after death")? Yes. From what I was shown, the other side is home and earth is just a place to test yourself. But, too, it was clear that we have more than one life on earth. From what I could see, we come back to earth whenever we need to test our growth under pressure, to see if we can actually live the lessons learned on the other side.

During your experience, did you encounter any specific information/awareness that God or a supreme being either does (or does not) exist? Yes. The beings in the Temple were definitely superior to me and filled with such unconditional love too.

During your experience, did you encounter any specific information/awareness that you either did (or did not) exist prior to this lifetime? Yes. From what I was shown, we have many lifetimes on earth.

During your experience, did you encounter any specific information/awareness that a mystical universal connection or unity/oneness either does (or does not) exist? Yes. It seems there is a deep connection between the other side and our earthly existence. And one thing clear was that we are ALL connected here too. It is just that our bodies' physical density dulls that knowledge.

During your experience, did you encounter any specific information/awareness regarding earthly life's meaning or purpose? Yes. Patterns, life benchmarks as an individual and life benchmarks as a world or large group, all with the purpose of seeing how we react and whether we have grown spiritually or not.

During your experience, did you encounter any specific information/awareness regarding earthly life's difficulties, challenges, or hardships? Yes.

During your experience, did you encounter any specific information/awareness regarding love? Yes. All of it was unconditional, no judgments whatsoever attached.

During your experience, did you encounter any other specific information/awareness that you have not shared in other questions that is relevant to living our earthly lives? Yes. Future events and possible outcomes. Choices by the majority must still be made to see where it is going to end up.

Did you have a sense of knowing special knowledge or purpose?
Yes. Again, patterns and a much larger picture and why, or the purpose of the events shown to me.

What occurred during your experience included content that was both consistent and not consistent with the beliefs you had at the time of your experience? My basically Christian molded background might have led to certain expectations...but none of my experience was near to what is taught. I could see how different religions might try to explain all that I saw and felt, but there was so much more than any of them promote. My experience was something of a conglomerate of many religions...though not following any specific doctrinal ideal or image. It is like all of them might have a piece of the whole...but not all. What became crystalline clear to me during these experiences is that the problem comes more in how man interprets religion than in the religion itself. What I saw was so much more than one religion. However, there also seemed to be purpose in all of the religions...people drawn to the ones that would help them most with whatever "theme" their life purpose happens to be in this lifetime.

How accurately do you remember the experience in comparison to other life events that occurred around the time of the experience?
I remember the experience more accurately than other life events that occurred around the time of the experience. Many of the world events were not even discussed when these experiences occurred. Yet, several have already come to pass, with more still to come. On a more personal level, I was promised a better life in the future compared to where I was at the time, and that has also been true.

Discuss any changes that might have occurred in your life after your experience. Wanting to live my life in a way that is worthy of that unconditional love I felt. That means always putting people first.

My experience directly resulted in: Slight changes in my life.

Did you have any changes in your values or beliefs after the experience that occurred as a result of the experience? Yes. Accepting of all people and where they are in life. All of us are still learning and it is okay. It is okay to make mistakes and we do not need to, nor should we judge each other. Each one is doing what they must do to continue the learning and testing they were put here to do.

Are there one or several parts of your experience that are especially meaningful or significant to you? Feeling unconditional love has impacted me most and continually wanting to be worthy of that.

Do you have any psychic, non-ordinary or other special gifts after your experience that you did not have before the experience? Uncertain. It much depends on how you describe psychic. I can tap into that other side whenever I really feel a need, but more than anything is a feeling of a great sense of gratitude for all being exactly as it should be.

Have you ever shared this experience with others? Yes. It took a few years, as it was deeply personal and I did not feel ready to share it with everyone.

Did you have any knowledge of near death experience (NDE) prior to your experience? Uncertain.

What did you believe about the reality of your experience shortly (days to weeks) after it happened? Experience was definitely real. I really needed time to sort it out and assess it all.

What do you believe about the reality of your experience at the current time? Experience was definitely real. I have heard scientific explanations about the thalamus and cortex of the brain shutting down and creating this experience. Maybe they are correct. However, it really doesn't matter to me whether they are or not. I had such a great experience that if death and all is an illusion, it does not matter. My experience was real to me and I feel I have purpose in living. What else matters?

Have your relationships changed specifically as a result of your experience? Uncertain. I don't really know. I love, but have always loved. If anything, I just try not to judge and maybe I was more prone to that before. I try to love others as unconditionally as I felt loved throughout the experiences.

Have your religious beliefs/spiritual practices changed specifically as a result of your experience? Uncertain. I do not feel a need to belong to any specific religion. I also do not feel the fear that religions seem to try to push on people. If that helps someone do the right thing and take care of others, through fear... great. But religion, in itself, is destined to always be interpreted by man. Their interpretations are often lacking real clarity and have a lot of falsities in place too. One of the things I was told, look always to "who benefits?" in rules made by religion. If it is particular men, or the power structure itself—chances are that it is not really something of God. Many rules are definitely man made and put there to benefit either the structure or those in charge of the structure.

At any time in your life, has anything ever reproduced any part of the experience? Yes. I can sometimes visit the city of God - by thinking about it. However, I rarely feel that need. Early on, I could also recreate that sense of unconditional love. After all these years, the intensity of it is not so easy. At the same time I do not have that same need of it that maybe I needed back then. I look forward to that love filling me once again, when I leave this particular life.

Did the questions asked and information that you provided accurately and comprehensively describe your experience? Yes. There was more to it, but I think my descriptions are sufficient.

Please offer any suggestions that you may have to improve this questionnaire. Are there any other questions that we could ask to help you communicate your experience? Not really.

THIRTEEN

Dr. Jan's experience is about a womblike void with unconditional love. Both, the changes in her life and the most meaningful part of the NDE were from the unconditional love she experienced on the other side. Although her experience wasn't remembered immediately upon waking, this is not uncommon. It doesn't diminish the reality or the effects of the NDE in her waking reality. I personally think that everyone has an experience when they die and come back, but it is only a few people who are allowed to remember the experience. Most of the reasons for a person to have a NDE seem to do with spiritual progress, and I think you will agree when you read this NDE, that Dr. Jan's experience had a profound impact on her spiritual progress and outlook on life.

DR. JAN

I was sitting next to my daughter when the rock larger than the tour bus fell on the back of the bus where we were seated. My daughter and I were asleep at the time. I knew immediately that I had a pneumo-thorax and would die unless someone recognized it. I also remember my teeth hitting together hard to the point some broke (which is what actually probably caused the concussion), but I was completely unaware of the hit on the head which caused the teeth to break. I was totally focused on myself and had no knowledge of my daughter. I was told I needed to stand up and get off the bus, but I said I couldn't. Then the person said I had to muster all my strength and get up. (the person has verified these words). I started to stand and then I remember nothing of my physical surroundings until I "woke up" on the x-ray table in the hospital in Cusco, 7 hours later. Yet I was told I was talking during the first part of the 7 hours.

I was not aware that I had lost consciousness until probably a week later and had no idea of the length of time between the accident and arriving in the hospital. At first I had no memory of what happened during those 7 hours, but when the memory returned it was extremely difficult. I was physically unable to hardly move and sleep because of the injuries and couldn't initially understand why I had to come back to this physical body. What I remembered was that I had completely merged again with God. It was a void, darkness, but unconditional love. I was no longer a separate being. I was where I belonged, where I came from. It was perfect. When it was time to return I had to again differentiate from God and become a separate soul again. Yet I was still a part of God. Then I was back on Earth in this physical body.

At the time of your experience was there an associated life-threatening event? Yes. I had bilateral pulmonary hemorrhages, a pneumothorax, concussion and multiple fractures on the left side. My blood pressure was dropping rapidly and my breathing slowed to only 4 times a minute. I was at an altitude of about 14,000 ft. I was told that I was cold and gray and the nurse felt like I was deciding whether to live or die.

Was the experience difficult to express in words? Yes. It is difficult to adequately convey the feelings.

At what time during the experience were you at your highest level of consciousness and alertness? Just after the accident before I lost my awareness. Supposedly I continued to speak but I have no memory after the accident for 7 hours.

How did your highest level of consciousness and alertness during the experience compare to your normal everyday consciousness and alertness? More consciousness and alertness than normal. I knew exactly what was wrong with my body. That continued for a few days after the accident as I drifted in and out of consciousness. But I felt no pain.

Please compare your vision during the experience to your everyday vision that you had immediately prior to the time of the experience. Everything was dark but I felt that I could see.

Please compare your hearing during the experience to your everyday hearing that you had immediately prior to the time of the experience. Same as normal.

Did you see or hear any earthly events that were occurring during a time that your consciousness/awareness was apart from your physical/earthly body? No.

What emotions did you feel during the experience? Exhilaration.

Did you pass into or through a tunnel? No.

Did you see an unearthly light? No.

Did you seem to encounter a mystical being or presence, or hear an unidentifiable voice? I encountered a definite being, or a voice clearly of mystical or unearthly origin.
    I encountered a definite presence that I would call "God".

Did you encounter or become aware of any beings who previously lived on earth who are described by name in religions (for example: Jesus, Muhammad, Buddha, etc.)? No.

Did you encounter or become aware of any deceased (or alive) beings? No.

Did you become aware of past events in your life during your experience? No.

Did you seem to enter some other, unearthly world? A clearly mystical or unearthly realm.
    It was a void, darkness but yet I felt it contained all light at the same time.

Did time seem to speed up or slow down? Everything seemed to be happening at once; or time stopped or lost all meaning. The void was outside of space and time.

Did you suddenly seem to understand everything? Everything about the universe
That we are one with God, we are God, just differentiated from God to get a physical body and come to Earth.

Did you reach a boundary or limiting physical structure? No.

Did you come to a border or point of no return? No.

Did scenes from the future come to you? Scenes from my personal future.
I didn't specifically remember this until a year later on the anniversary of the accident. I realized that I had traveled into the future to see my life to see why I should return because I did not want to come back to Earth. But I never recalled specifics. I felt at that moment like there was a wrinkle in time.

During your experience, did you encounter any specific information/awareness suggesting that there either is (or is not) continued existence after earthly life ("life after death")? Yes. We become one again with God, no separation. If our work is finished then we again merge with God. I had the sense that if our soul work isn't done that this merging doesn't happen. That was why other people had different near death experiences. I had reached the ultimate goal.

During your experience, did you encounter any specific information/awareness that God or a supreme being either does (or does not) exist? Yes. The void was God, all is God

During your experience, did you encounter any specific information/awareness that you either did (or did not) exist prior to this lifetime? Yes. I existed as God, then differentiated to become me in this life time. During the experience again I become one with God and had to differentiate again to become me once more.

During your experience, did you encounter any specific information/awareness that a mystical universal connection or unity/oneness either does (or does not) exist? Yes. We are all a part of God, originating from God.

During your experience, did you encounter any specific information/awareness regarding earthly life's meaning or purpose? No.

During your experience, did you encounter any specific information/awareness regarding earthly life's difficulties, challenges, or hardships? No.

During your experience, did you encounter any specific information/awareness regarding love? Yes. The void is unconditional love.

During your experience, did you encounter any other specific information/awareness that you have not shared in other questions that is relevant to living our earthly lives? Yes. Death is not to be feared. It is wonderful.

Did you have a sense of knowing special knowledge or purpose? Uncertain. Not initially, but as I relived the experience and asked the spirits why I had to return, the purpose became very clear. I needed to help others understand what lies for them after death so they won't be afraid. Also I help lost spirits cross over by finding the light (even though I do not recall seeing a light).

What occurred during your experience included content that was both consistent and not consistent with the beliefs you had at the time of your experience? I was surprised that I experienced darkness. But the unconditional love was consistent with beliefs.

How accurately do you remember the experience in comparison to other life events that occurred around the time of the experience? I remember the experience more accurately than other life events that occurred around the time of the experience. The hospital stay is less clear. The experience could have been today.

Discuss any changes that might have occurred in your life after your experience: I eventually quit my job and traveled back to Peru for months at a time to try to learn about the spiritual healing traditions there that had probably saved my life. My priorities have changed, I am much more open to where spirit directs me. I have complete trust in Spirit to direct my life in all areas. If I think I have control, it is only an illusion.

My experience directly resulted in: Large changes in my life

Did you have any changes in your values or beliefs after the experience that occurred as a result of the experience? Yes. I believe that we can heal ourselves, that we understand our body better than anyone else. I believe that we are not just a physical body, but an energetic and spiritual body. What happens on a spiritual and emotional level affects our physical body. If we are in balance in the spiritual and emotional bodies, then our physical body will be in good health. If we are out of balance then the physical body will become diseased.

Are there one or several parts of your experience that are especially meaningful or significant to you? The experience of unconditional and complete love is the most significant yet the most difficult to maintain here on Earth.

Do you have any psychic, non-ordinary or other special gifts after your experience that you did not have before the experience? Yes. I see and hear spirits, sometimes angels. When I do Tai Chi I often hear the voice of the deceased Master or the mountain spirits instructing me (sometimes softly, sometimes rather scolding). I understand the lessons from nature, such as the way a cloud is formed or the birds flying or the flowing of a river. I can connect with nature so that I can ask the wind to help me see the full moon by parting the clouds and it will happen.

More often the spirits play tricks on me. For example when I was in the middle of nowhere in Montana about to run out of gas and I asked for a gas station. Immediately there was a gas station but it was closed! So I asked for an open gas station. In a few minutes there was an open gas station but the first few pumps had no gas. Oh, come on!

Also I can talk with infants and children telepathically. I was visiting a pediatrician in Mexico when he said he had an interesting patient for me, a boy age 3 who wouldn't talk. They had run tests, even sent him to a specialist, but still didn't know why. But the boy "told" me that words were a waste of time and people should talk like he did, through their minds. Telepathically I told him that he really needed to speak because they would keep running tests on him. 2 days later I saw the doctor. He told me that the boy had returned because he was sick. But he verbally asked the doctor where I was and had started talking out loud! So when a sick child or infant comes to the office and I can't find what is wrong, I just ask and they often know.

Have you ever shared this experience with others? Yes. I was initially very angry that I needed to return here, so it wasn't until I was able to fully remember why I returned that I was able to share, probably about a month. No one truly understands. The ones that understand to some degree are those about to die or those that have a loved one about to die. Or those that have had a NDE.

Did you have any knowledge of near death experience (NDE) prior to your experience? Yes. I had read about the experiences, but most had seen loved ones that had passed on or a light. I didn't understand why my experience seemed so different.

What did you believe about the reality of your experience shortly (days to weeks) after it happened? Experience was definitely real. It was absolutely real. I had experienced the overwhelming love of the divine.

What do you believe about the reality of your experience at the current time? Experience was definitely real. When people don't believe in God, I say I don't have faith, I have experience. And I can't deny that experience.

Have your relationships changed specifically as a result of your experience? Yes. Relationships are based more on mutual spiritual quests. I don't have time for frivalous relationships.

Have your religious beliefs/spiritual practices changed specifically as a result of your experience? Yes. I spend more time in nature, especially in the mountains. The spiritual existence is what is most important in our life on this Earth. We aren't here necessarily to learn a lesson (although we do learn lessons when we stray off the path), but we are here to experience the joy of this place and the fellowship with all things.

I spend usually 40 minutes in chanting and meditation every morning and then yoga or Tai Chi before going to work. I was never that consistent before the accident.

At any time in your life, has anything ever reproduced any part of the experience? Yes. A shamanic exercise in the dying process brought back the memories.

Is there anything else that you would like to add about your experience? Before the accident I had downloaded some information about my upcoming trip to Peru, which was a spiritual journey. The information said that the rites we were to receive were the highest rites of the Incans and the lore was that the physical body could be recreated after death. I had the sense that I might die on the trip. I was sitting in my office about 2 weeks before the trip and made that same comment to my office mate. After he left I heard a voice saying that yes I might die and I had a choice about doing the work. I said I felt that the work was of the utmost importance and possibly could save the people of this world. I told no one about this and then forgot about it. Until the accident. As soon as the accident happened, I remembered the event but somehow knew I wasn't going to die. When I went back home and looked at the information that I had printed, there was no web address on the pages and I was never again able to find the website again despite entering the same search words.

About a year and a half later I returned to Peru. I met a shaman who read the coca leaves. He said I would come for 1-2 years to Peru to learn the Andean cosmology and healing traditions. I was a single parent with three kids - no way was that happening. I asked the spirits to release me from that path. Then three days later my friend in Peru who had had surgery started bleeding. Because I am doctor she asked for my help. But then she said that she thought the reason for the bleeding was because of something she had done wrong in her life. I was out of my league medically. So I asked for forgiveness from the spirits in asking out of my path and asked for help. I felt one of the mountain spirits come and sit on my shoulder like a bird and direct me in the healing. Then I saw him fly down and use it's beak to put in a stitch. Then it came back on my shoulder and told me to tell her she was forgiven and healed. I said I couldn't do that. So it repeated the command and again I said it didn't understand that I didn't have the power to do that. Then it said "Did you ask for my help?" so I told her three times she was forgiven and healed. Then my friend "woke up", said she was fine, and the bleeding did not return. So, I thought, "uh-oh, I think I am going to spend 1-2 years learning these ways". More like the rest of my life. It's difficult this spiritual path, but I wouldn't trade it for anything.

Did the questions asked and information that you provided accurately and comprehensively describe your experience? Yes.

FOURTEEN

egi's experiences typify the two most common ways of dying that we see in women and children, pregnancy or birth-related complications and drowning. When she had her first NDE as a child, she did not remember her drowning experience until much later in life. This is also a common theme in NDEs because information is blocked from memory if it will interfere with spiritual growth or lessons on earth. She had a lot of deep-seated rage issues as an unloved child, that came out when she had her second NDE and encountered God. While it is unusual to argue with God, it is not unheard of. Many NDErs return for the sake of their children. In fact, my research shows that one of the strongest reasons that people return to earth is for their children. The second NDE was the result of an ectopic pregnancy. Many times the life lessons on earth are about different aspects of love. Pegi came from an unloving family, yet was able to raise and foster so many children in a life of service, love and compassion.

One psychological aspect of NDErs is the tendency to dissociate. Although dissociation is a psychological term associated with the mind, NDE is a state of consciousness that deals with the soul. The soul appears to interface with different people in different ways. The NDE is medically inexplicable, so a psychological element may only explain part of what happens as the soul interfaces with the brain. I think the power of prayer is due to the brain/mind interfacing with the soul. The following account of Pegi saving her son through prayer is nothing short of amazing!

PEGI R.

As an adult of twenty-five.

While my husband was driving me to the emergency room an hour away, I was in severe pain. When we were almost there, the feeling of fading/dying came suddenly after the pain stooped. Once we got to the hospital, I told the nurse I was going to pass out or throw up. I also told her that I thought I had a tubal pregnancy. The nurse gave me a bowl in case I did throw up. Then she pushed me down a hall in a wheel chair. I leaned my head over the bowl as she pushed me along. I felt very sick and faint.

Suddenly, I found myself going very fast through a tunnel. The sound of wind as I sped through the air was loud. It was like being on a roller coaster, going straight up towards space. I shot upwards like a rocket and I could tell I was traveling a very long distance. I felt scared about where the tunnel might be taking me, thinking that I wouldn't know how to get back. It was clearly a feeling of leaving Earth and going way out to somewhere else in space. Then everything stopped. It was perfectly still and quiet. I was suspended in mid-air and completely surrounded by a bright light. Up, down, below and above me was all light—a white light. And I was inside the light. I couldn't see myself, but I still felt like me. I didn't know what to do. I was thinking about my new situation and recalling the tunnel and speed, and how it had abruptly stopped. "And now here I am," I thought to myself. I knew I had died.

At first I felt I was alone. Then I noticed shadows standing in front of me. The shadows formed a panel of people. They were looking at me. I could feel them and see their outlines. They were all standing, except one in the front middle who was sitting down. The one in the middle was God. God spoke to me, and I replied to him. I was rude and disrespectful. I started screaming that I didn't want to be there and didn't want to stay. I was very angry. I told him I have young sons at home that need me. I screamed, "I won't go!" Then God let me know, through thought, that I may be trying to get my way, but, I was not the boss there. So I humbled myself before him, and asked him to look into the future. I said, "If my sons would be better off without me, I will agree to stay." But if my sons would be worse off without me, I begged to go back to take care of them. God showed me sons at home who were being raised by their dad without me there. They were all so sad and alone. My husband had a girlfriend who didn't love them in the way I loved them. I could tell my sons missed me terribly. I was so sad and I longed to comfort them. I then asked God, "Who else will teach them about you?"

Suddenly, I was back in my body and still in my wheelchair. My head was still down, hanging limp over the bowl in my lap. The nurse pushing me was now chatting with another woman. First, I could only hear their voices. Then I started to feel my body. First I felt my hands on the wheelchair armrests, and then started to feel the rest of my body. I thought to myself, "That nurse doesn't even know her patient just died; because she was so busy socializing." Then I thought, "What the hell just happened?" and then, "I can't think about that now, I have to focus on staying alive and how I am going to survive this." I knew in my heart that the twins I was carrying were dead. I needed to find a way to stay alive for my sons at home. The nurse took me into an examination room, and put me on a tall examination table. I was shaking and freezing cold. My husband was there waiting for me. He held my knees down to keep me from shaking myself off the table. He had them continue getting me warm blankets. The doctor came and prepped me for a surgery procedure, but then said I didn't need it because the uterus was intact. He said I could stay overnight if it would make me feel better. My husband went home.

All night I was alone in a room. I would feel terrible pain in my right hipbone area (tube) then I would sit up, and pass out, and wake up covered in vomit. Every time I sat up, I would pass out and vomit while passed-out. The nurse got mad and said I needed to use my bowl, and refused to call the doctor. She said he was home asleep and she wasn't going to wake him. The next morning I had an ultrasound done. I was flat in my bed, because I would pass out whenever they tried to sit me up in a wheelchair. The ultrasound revealed my entire abdominal cavity up to my chest was filled with blood from internal bleeding. Then they saw that one baby was in my uterus and the other one was halfway in my uterus and the other half was stuck in my right ovarian tube. I was an organ donor, so they had me sign away all my organs one at a time to people in need of donated organs. Then they rushed me to emergency surgery. They called my whole family in and told them I wasn't going to survive. I overheard my mother taking charge of the funeral arrangements.

At the time of your experience was there an associated life-threatening event? Yes. Against my own wishes, at age twenty, I had had a tubal ligation. At age twenty-five, I had it reversed, so I could conceive. The next month I was pregnant with twins. But at seven weeks, I began having pain. By the end of that week, I could barely walk. I began bleeding and the pain became very intense. I knew it was a tubal pregnancy but my doctor wouldn't believe me. An ultrasound at that time, looked as if that both babies were in my uterus. But the ultrasound revealed that one baby was partly in my uterus and partly in my fallopian tube. This had caused so much bleeding that my entire abdominal cavity was filled with blood.

Was the experience difficult to express in words? Yes. The first time I told anyone was months afterwards. I told my husband. While telling him, I shook uncontrollably, just as I had at the hospital upon waking up. I could vividly feel the freezing cold from my experience. It seemed as if there was a struggle going on about telling my experience and getting it out of me. I felt like my body, or the fear in my mind, was fighting my soul's need to express itself. I was afraid my husband would laugh at me, think I was crazy, and tell everyone I was nuts and a liar. More importantly, I had my own fear of remembering the experience. Earlier that same day, before he got home from work, I had just started allowing myself to remember it. I couldn't seem to understand that it could have actually happened. But I KNEW it was true, and I had to tell someone. When I had finished telling my husband, he said he believed me. He knew me and could tell that by the way I looked when I told him, that I really had this experience. After that, each time that I got up the nerve to tell someone, I shook. But each time I would tell someone I shook less as my fear gradually went away. These days when I think about it, I'm no longer afraid. I mostly appreciate that I was allowed to come back and raise my sons. I don't fear death now, and I will accept God's will for me when the time comes. My sons are now grown. I KNOW there is Heaven and God, and there is nothing to fear about death. Only our body dies, but WE live on! I have such gratitude to God!

At what time during the experience were you at your highest level of consciousness and alertness? When I was in the tunnel and in heaven.

How did your highest level of consciousness and alertness during the experience compare to your normal everyday consciousness and alertness? More consciousness and alertness than normal. It was higher because I was so scared and begging for my life.

Please compare your vision during the experience to your everyday vision that you had immediately prior to the time of the experience. I seemed to be able to see all the way around myself without having to turn around.

Please compare your hearing during the experience to your everyday hearing that you had immediately prior to the time of the experience. I heard God and he heard me. We fully understood each other. My voice was speaking in words, and he communicated to my mind what he wanted to say. I experienced this communication as a male voice. It was a firm but loving voice. As I write this, I still hear/feel it. I had behaved like a spoiled child having a fit, kicking and screaming; he had been calm, but authoritative. He let me know I was not the one controlling this situation; he was. Yet I felt he surely would understand how much my children needed me. I finally trusted his wisdom, and placed my fate in his hands. I feel his fatherly love to this day. It comforts me and the memory and bond has not faded.

Did you see or hear any earthly events that were occurring during a time that your consciousness/awareness was apart from your physical/earthly body? No.

What emotions did you feel during the experience? I felt fear from so many things. Fear of not coming back. Fear of being so far away from my sons. Fear of my sons being told I had died and wouldn't be back. Fear of my sons needing me, and that I wouldn't be there to protect them and love them. I don't know if begging and pleading are emotions, but that sense of urgency is what I felt. I also felt resolve and sadness when thinking of not being able to return.

Did you pass into or through a tunnel? Yes. It was narrow. "Standing room only!" Round, long, it reminded me of a rope or a tube attaching to space. It was like a vacuum, sucking me/pulling me/shooting me way up and out, far away. The sound of speed and wind, hitting the sides of the tunnel as I passed through it made it was noisy. It wasn't dark, but it wasn't that light, either. Like a roller coaster, straight up to space.

Did you see an unearthly light? Yes. The light was a very, very bright white. It was everywhere and it was as if I was in a room made of light.

Light was the floor, the ceiling, the walls, up, down, middle—every-where, everything. And I was inside it, floating.

Did you seem to encounter a mystical being or presence, or hear an unidentifiable voice? I encountered a definite being, or a voice clearly of mystical or unearthly origin.

I saw God, I spoke to God. There were other people there, standing in a row behind him. God was sitting up front and center. I saw their outlines and sensed them all. (Imagine it is dark and you see that people are there, but it is too dark to make out who they all are—but you recognize the one in the middle of the front row as someone you know well). Only it was all white light instead of dark.

Did you encounter or become aware of any beings who previously lived on earth who are described by name in religions (for example: Jesus, Muhammad, Buddha, etc.)? Yes. God could have been Jesus. I refer to "God" when I speak of whom I was communicating with, but I wonder whether it might have been Jesus, instead—or if it matters.

Did you encounter or become aware of any deceased (or alive) beings? No.

Did you become aware of past events in your life during your experience? No. I did not forget my past, it just wasn't important to me compared to what was happening. Only my children's future was of importance to me.

Did you seem to enter some other, unearthly world? A clearly mystical or unearthly realm.

I was in Heaven and was talking to God. Other spirits were present, who listened but did not speak.

Did time seem to speed up or slow down? No.

Did you suddenly seem to understand everything? No.

Did you reach a boundary or limiting physical structure? Yes. I was bound against my will in the tunnel and in Heaven. It seemed the white light was contained in a room; meaning it did not go on forever.

It was more as if we were in a private meeting room at the entrance to Heaven. I sensed I would move on further, if I were to stay.

Did you come to a border or point of no return? I came to a barrier that I was not permitted to cross, or was "sent back" against my will. I was at "a point of no return" but WAS allowed to return. I was originally supposed to not go back.

Did scenes from the future come to you? Scenes from my personal future. I believe I saw what my sons' lives would be like if I couldn't return.

During your experience, did you encounter any specific information/awareness suggesting that there either is (or is not) continued existence after earthly life ("life after death")? Yes. I was told that I did not control my dying or living, it was up to God.

During your experience, did you encounter any specific information/awareness that God or a supreme being either does (or does not) exist? Yes. God did exist, I saw him, talked to him, argued with him, begged him, and reasoned with him. He allowed me to return. God let me know that I needed to settle down, and that I do not run things there; he does. The others were obeying him by allowing him to speak to me without their interrupting.

During your experience, did you encounter any specific information/awareness that you either did (or did not) know prior to this lifetime? No.

During your experience, did you encounter any specific information/awareness that a mystical universal connection or unity/oneness either does (or does not) exist? Yes. I told God that I knew he could look into the future and see if my sons would be better off without me. I told him that if my sons were going to be better off without me, I would stay there. He allowed us to look at the future to see what was going to happen if I didn't return.

During your experience, did you encounter any specific information/awareness regarding earthly life's meaning or purpose? Yes.

During your experience, did you encounter any specific information/awareness regarding earthly life's difficulties, challenges, or hardships? No.

During your experience, did you encounter any specific information/awareness regarding love? No.

During your experience, did you encounter any other specific information/awareness that you have not shared in other questions that is relevant to living our earthly lives? No.

Did you have a sense of knowing special knowledge or purpose? Yes. Knowing what God felt, and feeling he knew what I felt. There was no stumbling with words, all was open communication and well understood.

What occurred during your experience included content that was not consistent with the beliefs you had at the time of your experience.
I never imagined that I would go to Heaven and tell God off. I never thought you went kicking and screaming. I thought that fear of death was what came before death, and then once you're in Heaven it's all blissful and happy. I didn't know you could ask to come back to earth, and that some people do come back. I had never heard of "near death experiences" when I had mine. I did know from being Catholic that God is omniscient. I knew he can see into the future, and that's why I asked him to look.

How accurately do you remember the experience in comparison to other life events that occurred around the time of the experience?
I remember the experience more accurately than other life events that occurred around the time of the experience. I have never forgotten it: The memory has never faded, nor the feelings I felt. It is similar to PTSD, with strong emotional memory, but it is a good memory and makes me feel good. I love talking about it, and I control when I recall it. The memory is not intrusive or out of my control. But, the NDE is vivid like PTSD memories are: detailed and emotional. Life changing.

Discuss any changes that might have occurred in your life after your experience. At first, I just thought about what had happened, and

I was afraid of what people would think about me if I told them about it. Years later when I would talk about my NDE, I noticed people didn't seem to believe me or even care. In the last several years, as I get older and wiser, I care less what others think. I marvel at the experience. I remarried when I was 36. We adopted 9 children, after I had fostered 60 children in 16 years. My husband listens to me, and I know I can be open to him. He knows I am honest. He believes my experiences, so it allows me to explore them without judgment. When I pray now, I take myself to that light in heaven, and pray from there, face to face with God. I happily tell my story, and people can hear the truth and believe or not, it is up to them.

I do not fear death now that I have raised my sons. I feel such appreciation for my life being given back to me. I have brought my husband and adopted children into the church, and I am more spiritual now than religious. I do feel that I have healed people physically, emotionally and spiritually, because I think I brought a little bit of the light back with me. The light is healing. I have a little ESP. I feel that I levitate if I talk about God, heaven, or spirituality long enough. I sort of step out of my body a little. That was scary at first, too, but I have learned to not fear being slightly out of my body. One time, someone close to me died, and I touched them, I communicated with them, and explained things to them.

My experience directly resulted in: Large changes in my life.

Did you have any changes in your values or beliefs after the experience that occurred as a result of the experience? Yes. I used to "believe in" God, now I "KNOW" there is a God. I used to pray to someone far away, now I pray right in front of God.

Are there one or several parts of your experience that are especially meaningful or significant to you? The fact that God is as close to me as I need him to be. If you are afraid, open your hand and hold his—he is there. If you need an answer, pray and listen. The answer will come. If you hear his voice, it is a blessing.

Do you have any psychic, non-ordinary or other special gifts after your experience that you did not have before the experience? Yes. I had it before, but dismissed it. Now I recognize it more and I use it without fear. I see it as a gift from God now, and nobody else needs to accept it or believe it. It is helpful to me and others. My gifts provide depth and wonder to my life.

Are there one or several parts of your experience that are especially meaningful or significant to you? The fact that God is as close to me as I need him to be. If you are afraid, open your hand and hold his—he is there. If you need an answer, pray and listen—it will come. If you hear his voice, it is a blessing.

Have you ever shared this experience with others? Yes. But it was months before I told anyone. Then I only told my experience a few times with those people I thought I could trust to tell. It turned out that nobody wanted to hear it, so after that, I didn't tell anyone. Now I tell people if something about death comes up, but first I say, "I will tell you if you want me to." And usually they don't want to hear it. My husband and kids hear about it anytime I feel like talking about it, now.

Did you have any knowledge of near death experience (NDE) prior to your experience? No. When I first told my husband, Oprah's show was new, and she had had it on that day. I stood there in front of the TV, stunned, all alone, saying aloud, "It's real! That's what happened to me!"

What did you believe about the reality of your experience shortly (days to weeks) after it happened? Experience was definitely real. I knew it was real. I said, "What the hell was that!" to myself as soon as I was back in my body, but I told myself to push it aside for the time being, because I had other things I had to focus on, like staying alive. Not until I saw the Oprah show, could I even begin to put it into words and try to explain it.

What do you believe about the reality of your experience at the current time? Experience was definitely real. I have no doubt whatsoever about the reality of my experience.

Have your relationships changed specifically as a result of your experience? Yes. Years later, I had another tubal pregnancy. I knew the signs, and my doctor learned his lesson and listened to me. We caught it early. But as I laid there before surgery, I looked at my (now ex) husband, and told myself, "The next time I am on my death bed, I will have a different husband—one that cares." And we divorced soon afterwards. God led me to my current husband, and we are soul mates.

Have your religious beliefs/spiritual practices changed specifically as a result of your experience? Yes. I am more spiritual than religious now. I believe in God and I pray to God on a deeper level. I don't need to confess to a priest or to repeat rehearsed prayers. I talk to God and he is there. I go by how things feel. For me, it's not so much about the physical world with its objects and things any more.

At any time in your life, has anything ever reproduced any part of the experience? No.

Did the questions asked and information that you provided accurately and comprehensively describe your experience? Yes.

Please offer any suggestions that you may have to improve this questionnaire. Are there any other questions that we could ask to help you communicate your experience? Yes, ask if they ever attempted suicide to try to go back. I did once. I wanted to be with the babies I lost, after my sons were grown. God and heaven are so real after a NDE, this earthly life can look like just going on vacation. To go back is just through the veil.

As a child of five.

My mother, my sister Teri, and my brother John walked down the hill from our house to swim in the pond along SR 7 (State Road 7) on a hot sunny day. I went over to the water by myself to get in. I waded in to where I could still touch, because I couldn't swim like my four older siblings could. I was the youngest of five and could only dog paddle. I dog paddled around awhile, then came across a board floating in the water. I lay down on it and used it as a raft. It worked well and it didn't sink. So I used it to paddle clear to the center of the pond. I was so pleased with my accomplishment that I had to yell for my brother John to look at me. He was seven and a good swimmer. John quickly swam out to where I was, grabbed the board away from me, and took off with it, using it himself. I sank. I was kicking and screaming, trying to get my head above water. I was swallowing water and choking.

Suddenly I found myself under water, and I looked around—but I didn't know which way was up anymore, so I didn't know in which direction to kick. Up, down, and sideways all looked the same. The water was dark, and I couldn't see light anywhere. I was afraid if I kicked without knowing which direction to go, I might go deeper, instead of towards the surface. Or I might go sideways and never make headway, and I would drown. As I tried to think, I noticed I now WAS able to breath under water. I wasn't gulping water any more. I was fine! I thought my parents must have lied to me. They always said people can't breath under water, and I had to be careful or I could drown. I felt I hadn't drowned, because I was fine—I could breath under water just fine! In fact, it was wonderful! I was fascinated by it all! The water became beautiful—a shiny transparent light green. I saw fish swim right in front of my face. I looked closely at their fins, their mouths opening and closing as they wiggled along in the water. They bumped into my body and I thought it was strange, because we kids would try to catch fish with our bare hands when dad was fishing. We could never be quick enough to get a hold of the fish. They always got away. Now they acted like I wasn't a threat; like I was just an object in a fish tank or something else to swim around. Then I felt myself rising up in the water. I reached the top, and my vision seemed different.

I could see under water and over the water if I wanted. Like dipping a white egg in Easter egg coloring, two views of scenery at once. Or I could go up higher. After a while, I decided to go up higher. It was like I had choices of what I could see. I went up in the sky, and felt that was far enough for now. I could see my mom and sister Teri who was eight or nine at the time, sitting on a bed sheet on the bank, talking. I was very angry that they were so unconcerned that I had drowned, I felt, "I am dead and they don't even care!" I was jealous of their closeness and of not being included in their conversation. Then I saw on the opposite side of the pond from them, my brother John, on my board! I was so angry. Anger that I had never known before as a child, anger that a grown man might have—it was rage!

The next thing I recall, I was waking up. I was hanging over my brother John's right shoulder as he was carrying my body to the house. I saw, as I was hanging upside down, my mother and sister Teri walking up ahead, walking close together, and talking quietly, secretively. John said, "Mom, can I put her down now?" She glanced back at him, and saw I was vomiting water down his back. She nodded, "Yes," as she grabbed her chest in a sigh of relief, and turned back around and continued walking with Teri, crossing the train tracks, and heading up the hill to our house. End of memory.

At the time of your experience was there an associated life-threatening event? Yes. I drowned.

Was the experience difficult to express in words? No.

At what time during the experience were you at your highest level of consciousness and alertness? I was in the sky overlooking the pond and my family, and I felt rage because I had died, and my brother had caused it, and they hadn't even noticed or cared. I felt they should have been watching me. My brother knew I couldn't swim, but he took my board for himself. He didn't even need the board and I drowned without it.

How did your highest level of consciousness and alertness during the experience compare to your normal everyday consciousness and alertness? More consciousness and alertness than normal. Children generally don't feel that kind of rage and are not able to judge a situation like I did. And we certainly can't be suspended in water and enjoy the view without oxygen, nor choose to suspend ourselves in the sky and look down from that viewpoint without being on a limb of a tree or something.

Please compare your vision during the experience to your everyday vision that you had immediately prior to the time of the experience. Ability to see life from more different views than we can while alive. I was in such awe of the view underwater, it felt like seeing a miracle there.

Please compare your hearing during the experience to your everyday hearing that you had immediately prior to the time of the experience. I don't recall hearing anything, I was just seeing, feeling, and sensing the contentment of my family members, which caused me anger.

Did you see or hear any earthly events that were occurring during a time that your consciousness/awareness was apart from your physical/earthly body? Yes. While my body was underwater, I was above it, seeing what my family was doing, and seeing the pond from a bird's eye view.

What emotions did you feel during the experience? I felt fear, then I felt lost, then confused, then calm, then wonder/happy, then opportunity, then observation, then sadness and jealousy, then anger, then rage again.

Did you pass into or through a tunnel? No.

Did you see an unearthly light? No.

Did you seem to encounter a mystical being or presence, or hear an unidentifiable voice? No.

Did you encounter or become aware of any beings who previously lived on earth who are described by name in religions (for example: Jesus, Muhammad, Buddha, etc.)? No.

Did you encounter or become aware of any deceased (or alive) beings? No.

Did you become aware of past events in your life during your experience? No.

Did you seem to enter some other, unearthly world? Some unfamiliar and strange place. Not heaven, I was just was out of my body, in a different place, not a place of the living—a place of the dead.

Did time seem to speed up or slow down? No.

Did you suddenly seem to understand everything? Everything about myself or others.

I understood I was not loved or cared for by my family. I hadn't know that before. (And it became more apparent as I got older. Zero concern for me, still.)

Did you reach a boundary or limiting physical structure? No.

Did you come to a border or point of no return? No.

Did scenes from the future come to you? No

During your experience, did you encounter any specific information/awareness suggesting that there either is (or is not) continued existence after earthly life ("life after death")? Yes. I saw that we live on without the need for a body. Without our bodies, we can go where we want, and are able see people for who they really are. We can sum up situations without the need for the maturity of age. We can go places and marvel at parts of life that we are forbidden from seeing while living as a person on earth.

During your experience, did you encounter any specific information/awareness that God or a supreme being either does (or does not) exist? No.

During your experience, did you encounter any specific information/awareness that you either did (or did not) exist prior to this lifetime? No.

During your experience, did you encounter any specific information/awareness that a mystical universal connection or unity/oneness either does (or does not) exist? Yes. I could feel the thoughts and emotions of others; I didn't need to hear what they were saying because I could feel what was on their minds.

During your experience, did you encounter any specific information/awareness regarding earthly life's meaning or purpose? No.

During your experience, did you encounter any specific information/awareness regarding earthly life's difficulties, challenges, or hardships? No.

During your experience, did you encounter any specific information/awareness regarding love? Yes. I saw there was no love for me in my family, and it was a feeling of injustice that I drowned and that they did not even care.

During your experience, did you encounter any other specific information/awareness that you have not shared in other questions that is relevant to living our earthly lives? No.

Did you have a sense of knowing special knowledge or purpose?
Yes. I knew their feelings.

What occurred during your experience included content that was entirely not consistent with the beliefs you had at the time of my experience? I was only five. I did not think you could still be alive under water. I did not know what it was like to leave your body, or that you could, or that you could see and feel things while hovering over a pond.

How accurately do you remember the experience in comparison to other life events that occurred around the time of the experience? I remember the experience more accurately than other life events that occurred around the time of the experience. I did not remember this at all, until my early twenties. One night I sat alone outside and looked up at the stars in the night sky, to relax and get away from a stressful party at my in-laws' house. Suddenly I was very relaxed and amazed at the beauty of the night sky, then this memory crashed into my mind. Soon afterwards, I went to my mom's house, and asked her about it. Had I drowned when I was little in that pond? She looked at me oddly, as if she had forgotten all about it, and had just recalled it. She said yes, that I had, and said she thought it was another one of her kids that died that day. I wanted to know how they found me; was I floating or what? She couldn't recall. I went to my sister's house; she recalled it as well, but couldn't recall how they found me. I went to my brother's house, he said he remembers he got in a lot of trouble that day. Still he couldn't tell me, either, how they found me. That memory has not faded for me ever since the day it came crashing into my mind.

Discuss any changes that might have occurred in your life after your experience. I was five, so I don't know what I had thought either before or after my drowning. The memory came back to me in my early twenties, and then I was mainly curious about the facts surrounding the event, and making sure it was real. Now that I am older, I have assigned meaning to it. It reaffirms my belief that the soul does not die, but it does gain powers and abilities after it is free of our bodies.

My experience directly resulted in: Moderate changes in my life.

Did you have any changes in your values or beliefs after the experience that occurred as a result of the experience? Yes. Almost twenty years later, after I recalled it but it did not change me much until I had the second NDE when I was 25. The two experiences together have changed my life a lot—the second one more than the first.

Are there one or several parts of your experience that are especially meaningful or significant to you? The rage surprises me.

Do you have any psychic, non-ordinary or other special gifts after your experience that you did not have before the experience? Yes. I recall being around five or six and being punished by my dad. I had to sit on the toilet all night long until everyone got up the next morning. The ring from the toilet seat on my butt was getting sore, and I was bored. I wished I could go out the small window high up the wall, at the edge of the ceiling that was above the toilet. I wanted to sneak outside and go play. Then I did and later I came back to my body. I saw my spirit climb out the window, and after a time, climb back in. I couldn't recall what I did while I was out there.

When I was sixteen, I was kidnapped and raped. I knew my family would really hate me now for what "I" had done. I wished I were not even in this world, on this earth, because nobody on Earth loved me. Suddenly I was out in space, among the night sky and stars, looking at Earth from a distance. There was a light shining on Earth. It looked just like the globe looks, blue for the water areas, and land areas—a circle, suspended in air. (Just like our souls are after they die.) Then I came back to my body and the rape was over. I did not have to experience that happening to my body because of this ability that I have been given. Of course, I didn't understand being able to leave my body as a gift then, it was a wish-come-true at the time. When I got older and no longer feared recalling the rape and kidnapping, when I could talk about it without guilt, I understood it.

Have you ever shared this experience with others? Yes. After I recalled the drowning, I discussed it with my husband and mother and the two siblings involved. I have told some people since then—mostly people look at me like they think I am weird. I guess they think I am lying, even though I am known to be a very honest person.

Did you have any knowledge of near death experience (NDE) prior to your experience? No.

What did you believe about the reality of your experience shortly (days to weeks) after it happened? Experience was definitely not real, I assumed at age five, and I dismissed it.

What do you believe about the reality of your experience at the current time? Experience was definitely real. I know that memory is real, it came out of nowhere—it was very vivid and detailed and has not faded with time. If I had not recalled it, my family would never have told me about it. We are not close.

Have your relationships changed specifically as a result of your experience? Yes. Before I lost my twins due a tubal pregnancy (and NDE) I was pregnant with them on Easter Sunday. It was a beautiful sunny day, after a long winter and a lot of rain. We had purchased property, and my husband and I were standing on the spot where we were deciding to build our house. Our three little boys were playing in the woods, and they were near the creek. Suddenly my six-year-old Matthew screamed, "MOM! Jeremy!" We knew by his scream something awful happened to Jeremy. We could tell his scream came from the direction of the creek. My husband ran. Instinctively I knew, there was no time for me to run, I had to be there now. I stood frozen in fear, refusing to go see my son dead. I prayed to God, that he take my twins instead, and not my baby Jeremy. I said in my mind to Jeremy, in a prayer," Calm down, put your feet down, stand up." I knew he had fallen into the water, deep from all the rain, and that he had panicked, and was drowning. But it wasn't that deep.

As I stood in the bottom field, crying and praying, I saw Jeremy come up from the creek. He walked right past his dad, who had just reached the edge of the bank, and walk straight towards me, as if in a trance. His big blue eyes looked up at me and he said, "Was you worried about me, Mom?" I said, "Oh my God, Jeremy, you are my baby!" I kneeled down and hugged him and thanked God. Soon afterwards, I lost the twins. When Jeremy was an adult, I told this story for the first time. Jeremy was having a New Year's Eve party at his house. I was telling his friend and cousin about it. Jeremy overheard me telling it and he said, "I remember that!" I looked at him—I was shocked. I said, "You do!?" and he replied "Yes, when I was drowning, I heard you praying. I heard you tell me to not panic, to put my feet down." He said, "That's what it was—the water wasn't that deep, but I panicked and thought it was a lot deeper than it really was. I was trying to swim instead of just walk out of there." His friend replied, "That is a mother's love, right there!"

Have your religious beliefs/spiritual practices changed specifically as a result of your experience? Uncertain. Even though I didn't recall my drowning until I was grown, at about the same age as the drowning, I recall being in pre-Sunday school, and suddenly bursting into a strong feeling of the spirit. I started singing real loud and praising God! The other kids covered their ears and begged the teacher to make me stop. I had been very full of the spirit during that whole Sunday class, and I just couldn't contain it. My teacher told them, no, I was full of the spirit, and to let me be. (That was a one-time event.)

At any time in your life, has anything ever reproduced any part of the experience? No.

Did the questions asked and information that you provided accurately and comprehensively describe your experience? Yes.

FIFTEEN

Laura's NDE is nothing short of amazing! Laura had three sons. She" had just given birth to the fourth son when she hemorrhaged and "died." The interchange between Laura and the higher being has to do with free will and how she wanted to stay with Him. There is a marvelous discussion about love and the reason we come to earth. She talks about how we chose our parents and even our DNA lineage to complete our missions on earth. What is most remarkable, is that each person contributes in their own way to the collective unity of God. Notice how she was not allowed to remember her life review until it would not interfere with her mission in life.

LAURA M.

On May 18, 1970, the day my first son was born, I had serious medical complications that led to a serious post-partum hemorrhage. I received several blood transfusions.

I had an out of body experience where in I witnessed the birth of my son. I watched the doctor tell my husband that he could save the baby, but that I was going to die. From my vantage point at the top of the ceiling, I started screaming at them that, "I Am not Dead!!" They couldn't hear me. I was terrified! Then I witnessed my own funeral and burial. Afterwards, everything went Black.

It took three days before I could actually communicate and consciously respond to my surroundings. I knew that I was terrified of dying. I decided this awful experience was due to drugs. It took me years to get over it!

Fast forward to July 1979. Ten days after delivering my fourth son, I began hemorrhaging again. My husband rushed me to the hospital where I received several more blood transfusions and surgery to stop the bleeding. I woke up in the recovery room feeling fine. With encouragement from me, my husband went back to work with a promise that he would return in a few hours to take me home. I dosed off, only to wake up as my father entered the room. He lived 90 miles away and his visit was a happy surprise. He bent over to kiss me and I felt a shudder run through my body. Just nerves I thought. But then my teeth started to chatter and I began to have uncontrolled spasms. My temperature spiked and I was burning up. My father ran to get help and the medical personnel came running in the room.

A plastic sheet was thrown over my body and then someone started dumping buckets of ice on me. The pain was intense. I felt every piece of ice as if it were a knife piercing my burning flesh. Then my doctor appeared. I heard the nurse say, "I can't get a pulse, her temp is over 106. Her organs are shutting down!" I looked up at my doctor and told him that I was bleeding again. He replied, "No, you are having an allergic reaction to the blood transfusions you received." "No," I thought, "He doesn't know. I am hemorrhaging. Me! I am dying and my spirit is Flowing Out!" I felt overwhelming sadness. I was sad to be dying without saying "goodbye" and "I love you" to my husband, children, and my Father who was standing right outside the door.

And then, I Died! The first awareness I had was the absence of Pain. What a relief! Then I became aware of the Blackness. It was as if I was in a place of TREMENDOUS ENERGY. It was a great Black Void but I was not fearful. The Void held me in calm and peace. I knew I had died to the world, but I had not lost consciousness for even a second. I was still Me and still alive.

Then I was with HIM. I was enveloped in such a Great light and love that defies Description. I Rested in Joy, Bliss and Grace! He spoke to me saying that it was not my time and that I needed to return to my body in order to complete my life's mission. I had Clearly Heard and understood every unspoken Word! I asked Him how he had spoken to me without Words and without a Voice? He said to me that I was in a different place; one in which communication was Purely Exchanged through the Language of Love. Here everyone spoke Heart to Heart and Soul to Soul, so that there could never be a misunderstanding.

He reminded me again, that it was not my Time and that I needed to return to my body to resume my earthly life. Then I told Him that He had Promised Me Free Agency, and I was choosing to exercise that Agency to Stay With Him. He Laughed with Great Joy and Mirth at my stubbornness. He said, "Yes, Laura, I would Expect you to argue for your Own Case. The decision will, of course, be yours. But, first let me Show you some things." I was Suddenly Struck with Wonderment and Awe. He KNEW ME, EVERYTHING ABOUT ME WAS ALREADY KNOWN! I WAS PART OF HIS CREATION. IN ME WAS THE SPARK OF GOD. IT COULD NOT BE OTHERWISE. HE WAS ALL KNOWING. HE WAS ALL LOVE; AND I WAS A PART OF IT ALL!

Before me appeared a Pristine, Beautiful white, Glistening Beach. I Saw my Three oldest Sons sitting together on that beach. Individually I saw many parts of their future lives. I saw their Struggles and their hardships. I saw how my Death would add to their hardships. I was shown that sadness, loneliness, and anger seemed to surround them often. Then I saw the contrast if I chose to remain in their lives. My sons paths were lightened because of my love for them.

But still I could not imagine leaving Him and Being parted From His Love. I pointed out to Him the beach and how there were millions of each single grain of sand. Surely, one small grain of sand in all of creation would not be So Missed. I rationalized that my sons had a Wonderful, Loving Father to care for them, teach them, and LOVE THEM! Also I had realized that Time was different than on earth and did not really matter. After all, as a Mortal, how do you understand Forever? Eternity? No End? Life may appear Long, Hard And Dreary but in reality, it was a Flash in Eternity. My life was equal to one grain of Sand on that expansive Beach. He brought my focus back to the Beach explaining, "Notice again, the Beach with Every Individual Grain of Sand. Notice How Each grain touches Every other grain. If every individual gain of sand chose to remove itself, there would Be No Beach." I got it on All levels instantly! No one could replace me or anyone else! Ever! Everyone must contribute to their own unique part of the Beach.

Suddenly, it dawned on me that I had only witnessed the lives of three of my sons. "Where is my Baby?" I asked, "Why is He separated from his Brothers?" "He is younger. He will be raised differently," was the reply. "That cannot be," I said. "His Father would not let that happen." "His Father will not be with him long." I was given to understand.

"His Father will not have the influence on him as he does on your other sons."

I was shown that my husband would lose his life in an accident. (I was not allowed to remember this memory, but somewhere in the corner of my mind, it remained. I would remember it vividly four years later as my husband lay dying.)

The Focus again fell on my infant son and hundreds, if not thousands of my ancestors. I was aware of light surrounding many of them as they stood out. I felt Tremendous Love from them. He said, "Notice Your ancestors. All these Beings came together in Your Behalf to Make You Uniquely You." I realized in Earth words, He was referring to my DNA. "You wanted to go to earth to learn, to progress, to contribute to Creation. All these spirits came together to help You Do That." The focus then was back to my Baby. "In All of Creation," He said, "Your Infant Son Chose YOU to Be His Mother. None Other! Together, You made a Covenant to fill these rolls in each other's Earth Life. This Covenant is and Was a Very Sacred Covenant, Not to Be Taken LIGHTLY!" Suddenly I could not Wait to return to Earth and to all four of my sons. I wanted to return to my Family and to life on Earth. But before doing so, I was brought to another level of Awareness.

It was as if when I was Focused on Him, that it was my complete and only Awareness. When changing focus, l saw much more. My life flashed before me and I had a life review. When the review was over, my head was hung in Shame for HE had Seen it too. I was not happy about Many, Many of my Actions! I turned to Him asking, 'How could you Still Love me So Completely after witnessing my many sins?" "You are a Child of God," He Said, "and God Is Love—I see you Purely as Love." There Was No judgment, only Love was coming from Him. In order for Me to Understand this, I Needed to Forgive myself and Realize that I was a Part of Divine Love. Through the Atonement this was made possible. (Very difficult to explain). I remembered nothing that I saw in my life review. I only have the memory of having a life review and from that, Only the Love remains!

I then focused on my surroundings and I became aware of a Flower. It was a magnificent Flower, much like a perfect Gerber Daisy that was glowing in Brilliant Orange-hued colors. It was Alive and it was Loving Me. In Amazement, I turned again to Him in Wonderment And Awe exclaiming, "This Flower is Loving Me, I Can Feel It." "Everything," He said, "was Made in Love For You!" Then I Saw and Felt All. It was

Me and I was the Flower. I felt Colors – Alive, Loving, and Stunning Colors of Light. I felt the Water where each Drop was Alive and Loving. All this was communicated with No Words!

It was time to return, but first I had One more Question. "Why me?," I asked, "What made Me So Special that I was allowed to have This Happen to Me?" "Nothing," He replied, "Love Falls on Everyone Equally. Everyone Is Special. This was just something you Needed to accomplish your chosen life mission."

I was almost ready to return, but first I needed to Secure a Promise that I could Soon Return to Him! Again, I felt His Great Mirth, Tremendous Love for me, and His complete Knowing of me. He told me that There Really Is No Other Option; We All Return! He did remind me that the only thing I get to bring back with Me is Love; The Love I Gave Away on earth to others.

At the time of your experience was there an associated life-threatening event? Yes, hemorrhaging.

Was the experience difficult to express in words? Yes. There are No words in Any language on this earth, to explain. The Communication was Complete through Heart, mind, and Spirit. It was pure Love. I asked why communication was Not through Spoken word? I was told that Words on earth are misunderstood. There, I was communicating spirit to spirit and heart to heart; through the Pure language of Love and God. That way misunderstandings could not happen.

How did your highest level of consciousness and alertness during the experience compare to your normal everyday consciousness and alertness? More consciousness and alertness than normal. I was aware of Tremendous Energy! Aliveness. Everything was Connected, Alive and Held together with Love. There was Not even a remote possibility that I could Not Exist!

Please compare your vision during the experience to your everyday vision that you had immediately prior to the time of the experience. There was No vision as we know it on earth. There was Total Awareness of All. Not that I didn't see, because I Did. It was as if all the senses were heightened. This is difficult to explain, Like when you have a Very Vivid Dream, Your Eyes are closed but you See!

Please compare your hearing during the experience to your everyday hearing that you had immediately prior to the time of the experience. Hearing Again was through heightened Awareness. Although, there were No Spoken Words, I could still hear. I Heard and Felt the Harmony of the Universe—Like Music, but on a Soul Level. Again, it was pure LOVE.

Did you see or hear any earthly events that were occurring during a time that your consciousness/awareness was apart from your physical/earthly body? Uncertain. That is hard to answer because once I left, I chose to disconnect from my body and surroundings. I Could have been Aware had I Chosen to do so at any time! I was always aware, just not focused in that arena.

What emotions did you feel during the experience? LOVE - JOY - AWARENESS - COMPLETENESS - ENERGY - CONNECTEDNESS TO ALL - PERFECTION OF LOVE

Did you pass into or through a tunnel? No.

Did you see an unearthly light? Uncertain. I was aware of Total Light.

Did you seem to encounter a mystical being or presence, or hear an unidentifiable voice? I encountered a definite being, or a voice clearly of mystical or unearthly origin. I was melted into an Embrace of such Pure Love and welcoming Joy and Peace, that there are No Words to describe it. Words were not used but I Plainly Heard!

Did you encounter or become aware of any beings who previously lived on earth who are described by name in religions (for example: Jesus, Muhammad, Buddha, etc.)? Yes. I KNEW I was with JESUS. Though I cannot tell you What He looked like because he was total Light, I was Very Aware I was in His Embrace of Pure Love and Light.

Did you encounter or become aware of any deceased (or alive) beings? Yes. I was aware at some point of my progenitors. I was aware of Hundreds of them. It was explained to me that I had Chosen to come to Earth to complete a Certain Mission. The Mission was unique to Me but also had a Universal impact. I needed a specific DNA to complete my mission and my ancestors had united in Love to give that to me. There were No mistakes in my birth. Universal Perfection.

Did you become aware of past events in your life during your experience? Yes. I had a life review which caused me to 'Hang my Head' (what Head?) in shame because 'He' had seen it too. Then I turned to Him in amazement and asked, "How could this Be? You Saw my Life and Yet Your Love for Me did not waver or Change?" He replied (in essence), "You are a child of God and God is Love! You are a Part of God and God is Love. God knows only Love! But for You to understand this, you must forgive yourself, your human failings, and see yourself as God sees you - Which is Only As Love!" I only remember that I Had a life review and that Love is 'All'.

Did you seem to enter some other, unearthly world? A clearly mystical or unearthly realm. I was aware that I was in another Realm, although it is not necessarily a Place.

Did time seem to speed up or slow down? Everything seemed to be happening at once; or time stopped or lost all meaning. Time did not exist. How do you describe forever? Eternity? No End? Timeless?

Did you suddenly seem to understand everything? Everything about the universe. EVERYTHING MADE COMPLETE SENSE. I GOT IT!!

Did you reach a boundary or limiting physical structure? No.

Did you come to a border or point of no return? No.

Did scenes from the future come to you? Scenes from my personal future.

I did not want to return to earth. I reminded Jesus (haha, even He laughed in great joy at my reminding Him) That He had Promised Me Free Agency and I was Choosing to hold to that Promise and Stay with Him. He said Free Choice was mine. Nevertheless, maybe He could help me make a more informed Choice by showing me some future events in the lives of my children, and how my death would forever affect them. I communicated to Him that my Sons had a wonderful father that could take my place. He showed me my Husband's Death.

I was shown that my Sons would be orphaned at a young age. It was then through Great Compassionate, caring, and love for my Sons that I Chose to return. I did not remember Seeing my husband's death once I came back, but I Knew that something very Profound had been shown to me to encourage me to return to my body. Four years later, my Husband died as a result of an accident. During the time he was dying, the part of my NDE that I had forgotten was shown to me again.

During your experience, did you encounter any specific information/ awareness suggesting that there either is (or is not) continued existence after earthly life ("life after death")? Yes. I was always Aware of my continued existence. I was aware of my progenitors.

During your experience, did you encounter any specific information/awareness that God or a supreme being either does (or does not) exist? Yes. I knew that I was in the Presence of God! I was very surprised at the form of communication as I heard words, but No Words were Actually Spoken. I Asked, "Why? What form of Communication are we using?"

During your experience, did you encounter any specific information/awareness that you either did (or did not) exist prior to this lifetime? Uncertain. Before my NDE I had thought about reincarnation. Upon returning, I felt there was truth in it some way. Not Certain What. Maybe Universal consciousness, cellular memory from my Ancestors? Past lives? Parallel lives, as time is non-existing? I no longer feel 'Singular' so to speak.

During your experience, did you encounter any specific information/awareness that a mystical universal connection or unity/oneness either does (or does not) exist? Yes. I became Aware of a Beautiful Flower. It bent toward me and I could Feel love. The Flower was Alive with Energy and Love. It was like a Big Gerber Daisy: Brilliant, glowing, orange. I could feel it had intelligence. I commented in Awe that this Flower was Alive and Loving me. I was told that everything was created in Love for me. Then I became Aware of the Universal connection, love and oneness of All Creation.

During your experience, did you encounter any specific information/awareness regarding earthly life's meaning or purpose? Yes.

As in the above description of the Beach scene, I realized that We are each on an individual mission of Growth, learning, understanding, experiencing and Enjoying. But just as it is Individual mission, it is ALSO Universal because We all individually and collectively add to Creation and expansion of Earth. Everyone Touches, Everyone Contributes, Everyone Is Connected!

During your experience, did you encounter any specific information/awareness regarding earthly life's difficulties, challenges, or hardships? Yes.

During your experience, did you encounter any specific information/awareness regarding love? Yes. As I was about to return, He reminded me "Remember, Laura, that the ONLY THING YOU GET TO BRING BACK WITH YOU WHEN YOU 'DIE' IS LOVE. LOVE IS THE ONLY THING THAT IS REAL!"

During your experience, did you encounter any other specific information/awareness that you have not shared in other questions that is relevant to living our earthly lives? No.

Did you have a sense of knowing special knowledge or purpose? Yes. There is No Death. I have Been, and Will Always Be, A Part of God. As such, I Am Love.

What occurred during your experience included content that was both consistent and not consistent with the beliefs you had at the time of your experience? I Hoped that there was life beyond Death because I was taught that as a child. Now I KNOW there is No Death. There was not One Second in which I did Not Exist as Laura. I became Spiritual, Not Religious. There was So Much more than I Could Ever Have Imagined! I also got a Glimpse of the Perfection, connection, Love of all things and for a moment UNDERSTOOD everything.

How accurately do you remember the experience in comparison to other life events that occurred around the time of the experience? I remember the experience more accurately than other life events that occurred around the time of the experience. My remembrance has expanded as events in my life have taken place, like flashbacks almost. As when my Husband was dying, I fell asleep at the foot of his bed and a memory flooded me that was so stark and Real that it could not be denied. I knew I had seen the events around his Death when I had my NDE.

Discuss any changes that might have occurred in your life after your experience. I look at life much differently. I am open-minded when it comes to organized religion I cannot subscribe to Any one religion. I feel Deeply Connected to All of humankind. God is LOVE. There is No Such thing as a Judgment from God. His Love Is Unconditional. We are All a part of God and Each Other. There is No Greater, There is No lesser, because We are One. Love is All there Is! God Resides in Me. Since my return I can feel The Spark whenever I Pause to do So because It is Universal.

My experience directly resulted in: Large changes in my life.

Did you have any changes in your values or beliefs after the experience that occurred as a result of the experience? Yes. Greatly opened my mind. God does Not Judge.

Are there one or several parts of your experience that are especially meaningful or significant to you? All of them!

Do you have any psychic, non-ordinary or other special gifts after your experience that you did not have before the experience? Uncertain. I Seem to have moments of Awareness. Sometimes I Know Stuff and Have Dreams that come true. I do not have Any Fear of non-Existence. Unusual experiences have happened to me.

Have you ever shared this experience with others? Yes. After many, many years, I slightly mentioned it in passing sometimes. I have been doing Hospice for seven years and mention it often. Since 2001, my NDE has guided my Life almost entirely!

Did you have any knowledge of near death experience (NDE) prior to your experience? No.

What did you believe about the reality of your experience shortly (days to weeks) after it happened? Experience was definitely real. I was in shock! I tried to tell my doctor, but he didn't want to hear it. I had felt alone and I did not know how to explain it. I did not think anyone would want to hear it or really believe me. When I read Dr. Raymond Moody's book I was greatly relieved. I never denied the Reality of the experience, because I Knew it was Real! There were too many unknown things were explained to me.

What do you believe about the reality of your experience at the current time? Experience was definitely real. No change, It Happened; It was Real. I know I was meant to Share it in the work I was Chosen to do!

Have your relationships changed specifically as a result of your experience? Yes. I look at life differently. Very open minded. I expect Guidance. I know that I am Never, Never Alone! I am more tolerant of all people and life. I feel a sacredness to all of creation.

Have your religious beliefs/spiritual practices changed specifically as a result of your experience? Yes. I do not adhere to any specific organized religion. I am Me. Whatever that is, I call it spiritual. I Feel deeply connected!

At any time in your life, has anything ever reproduced any part of the experience? Yes. As mentioned earlier when my husband was dying as a result of an accident. Also, this may sound strange, but when I Saw the movie "Contact" with Jodie Foster, chills began to run down my spine. When she was drifting in space, the colors of the Sky, the Expansiveness of the Universe appeared, I could not stop the tears from flowing down. Nothing compared to what I Saw, but these sparked a flash of memory.

Is there anything else that you would like to add about your experience? When I had my NDE, it was difficult to process it. Then I read Dr. Moody's book. I vowed that someday I would meet him. I was so grateful and wanted to thank him. We shared the same last name; I thought that was Awesome. Fast forward to 2001. Through a Very Strange series of Events, I found out that he was teaching at a college in Las Vegas. I was living there at that time, so I called him. He invited me to speak to a couple of his classes. Before I went to speak, an even stranger sequence of events occurred. I found the story of one of my ancestors who had also had a NDE and written about it in 1900. All of this led me to sell my Recycling Company and then pursue a career as a Hospice and Grief Counselor. Now I tell my story whenever it seems Needed for my patients or their family.

Did the questions asked and information that you provided accurately and comprehensively describe your experience? Yes. I have not written the narrative completely, but I have described a great deal of it. This format was wonderful!

SIXTEEN

Sarah's experience is a probable NDE, because it isn't clear if she actually died. However, the distinction between NDE or Probable NDE is just for scientific classification purposes. What really matters is how remarkable this experience is and how spiritually transformative that it is.

I've said for a very long time that the NDEs are spiritual. Jesus demonstrates total, unconditional love and acceptance. It is as if religion tells you about a two dimensional being from a book, but the NDE gives Jesus much more depth and feeling.

This NDE is also remarkable in that many of the descriptions, like how she saw herself, is exactly what it would be like in a 4th dimension or greater universe. For instance, to have 360 degree vision (spherical vision) and to be looking at herself from three different perspectives is a wonderful description of showing the body is outside of our three dimensional reality.

The contrast in her miserable earthly life, what she had been taught as a Jehovah's Witness, and what she experienced on the other side makes this experience one of the best examples as to why people change from their experience. She saw how good her life would be when she returned. She came back with the remembrance of her mission - Love and have fun!

SARAH W.

At age 14, my leg was cut open from an accident. I was rushed to the hospital by ambulance. When I was hit, I saw my whole life play backwards in seconds. It was like watching a movie except the speed was super-fast. Every detail of my life was played back on that screen. During this time, I was thinking of all the people I loved and was sorry for being mean to anyone. Time seemed to slow down and almost stopped. I thought I was going to die and asked God, "How could I die when I don't have even one happy memory?" I thought, "What a sorry existence and a waste of creation. To die so unhappy with no happy memory." I was so angry that I didn't have a happy memory. I was abused as a child, unloved, and unwanted. It was a really crappy childhood.

After getting to the hospital, I was bleeding in the waiting room for 4 hours. By the time my Father ripped back the curtain and pulled a nurse over, I was covered in blood from head to toe. My kneecap was hanging out and I needed to get into surgery fast. I had X-rays and from there went into surgery. I was given anesthesia to put me under.

I was afraid that something was going to happen while I was under. I remembered my Grandfather had woken up during surgery and they weren't done operating on him yet. It's always stuck with me even to this day. I sucked in as much gas as I could because I didn't want to wake up during surgery. I thought I would just go to sleep and maybe dream. Well, I never lost consciousness and started freaking out. I was screaming and throwing myself all around. But, I wasn't really moving or yelling out loud. I was saying, "I am still awake!!"

The next second I realized that I was on the ceiling. I was completely calm and it was peaceful. I wondered why I could see the ceiling so well and so close up. I was weightless and seemed to be almost bouncing from the ceiling to floor. I heard and felt a super high pitch noise. It was painful to hear and I wanted to leave the area. As soon as I expressed discomfort, I was BOOM - in a black space. It was blacker than black and all void. I have always been afraid of the dark and thought maybe something would get me from out of the dark. I tried to feel my body and I didn't have one. I thought I was dreaming and I didn't understand why I couldn't feel my body. I wondered what I looked like since I didn't have a body. I tried to touch myself. My hands, or what I sensed as hands, went right through myself. I wondered where the light was and where my Father was. I didn't like being in the dark and wanted to find a light switch or something. I thought it would be pointless to try to move around if I couldn't see where I was going. I wanted to get out of the blackness, thinking maybe something would get me. I didn't see or sense danger at anytime in my experience.

I became uncomfortable and very concerned about where the light and my Father was, I saw a pin prick of light far off. In a flash, the light was coming right at me. I was an abused child and I got hit a lot. I was afraid the light was going to hit me in the face. I moved out of the way in fear of being hit. I turned around and saw this magical light full of color (gold, white and pinks all the colors together), like a diamond that has all the colors and sparkles. It seemed to be alive and calling me into it. I put my hand in first and it felt so incredible; my mind can't express in words the feelings of immense LOVE I felt. I put the rest of what I sensed to be my body into the light. I was literally and emotionally in LOVE as I became ONE with the light. I was held immediately so close and tight. It felt like someone was hugging me. I was thinking that I never wanted to leave the light because I thought the feeling would go away.

I never went back in the blackness. I allowed my walls to come down for the first time in my life. I allowed myself to get lost in the experience. I danced in the light and spun around. I was so happy to have felt good for the first time in my life. I wondered what I looked like since I couldn't see or feel myself in the void. I got a 360 degree view of myself but I only saw myself from the shoulders up. I looked the same as I always had. I thought, "Oh well, I look the same."

I saw two white lights coming from a far and they were the shape of people. I thought the medicine was making me not see clearly. I kept trying to blink and blink again to see if it was just me seeing them like this. I never saw detail. They remained white light beings. That is the best way I can describe them. They came to me and I said, "I couldn't see you very well. Do you know where my Father is?" They pointed and told me telepathically that he was at the end of the light. I asked if they would come with me because I couldn't see very well. They agreed and cautiously walked to the end of the light. I was almost inching my way because I didn't know what was on the other side of the end of the light. I asked them what was on the other side and they told me I had to go in to find out. I was afraid the feeling I was feeling of Love and hugs would go away if I went in. But, I trusted the two white light beings.

I went into what felt like a doorway. But, the light was so bright that I couldn't see past it or into it. I mean the light didn't hurt my eyes at all. I just couldn't see pass it to see the other side. When I passed through the doorway, I was now watching myself have this experience. I had three different perspectives of myself, as well as a 360-degree view of everything.

I saw myself ascending up into the huge like border of clouds. I went up into it and came to a place I could only describe as a world of lights. Everything was sparkling and glittery, like diamonds! Everything was alive with light and glowing. The trees, every living plant, and flower was pristine. There were no dead leaves or twigs from the trees or bushes. Everything was so clean and pristine. I walked, for what seemed a long while on this path or street, just looking around at how beautiful everything was. I came to a crossroad.

There was a building to the left of me. It was made of clear crystal-like material. The building seemed to go into the ground and came up at the coolest angle. I remember thinking, "Whoa, that is so cool!" I saw that there were 12 clear crystal walls or foundations. There were names written on them in different colors. They were English names because I could read them. I don't remember the names now. But, I do remember saying to myself that I needed to remember this. I stared at it for what seemed like a long while.

I could see ahead of me that there were two women coming in my direction. I was scared to talk to anyone. I didn't know where I was or where I was allowed to go. So, I tried to hide behind a tree as not to be seen. As they approached my direction, I tried to get as close to the tree as possible. I was able to go inside it. I was totally excited about this! I said "Oh, whoa, I always thought I could do this." I watched as the two women passed as if they couldn't see me. I just stood in this tree for so long it seemed. I was just happy to be in it. I thought the colors of the inside of the tree looked like the colors I was made of.

I heard playful male voice ask me, "Are you gonna stay in the tree the whole time?" I giggled and said, "Oh no, I didn't think I could go anywhere else." The voice said, "This is your HOME and you can go anywhere you wish." I said, "Really?" He replied, "Yes!"

I started walking down this street and then started doing gymnastics down the road. I have loved gymnastics ever since I was little. I was doing them perfectly! I have never done anything perfectly. It was like I had my eyes closed and was just following someone doing all these gymnastics. I remember walking into what I would call an office or room. The view was so beautiful! It was Earth stunning as she is in all her beauty. The water was so deep Blue it was incredible! There was a wall or window floor to ceiling. Just like the other material the other building was made of. It could have even been the same build. I was so busy dancing and doing gymnastics, I didn't pay attention.

The space around Earth was just like it is now, Black! It was the only time I saw anything dark up there. I was just staring out this see-through wall onto Earth. I was thinking about everything I had been through up to that point in my life and reflecting on the horrible things I have been through. I always said the same things in my mind over and over growing up, "Why wouldn't God protect me from being abused? Didn't I love him enough? Might he help me like the people in the Bible? Why he doesn't stick up for me?" I didn't think anyone liked me or loved me in this world. Over and over in my mind I would ask things like this. This time when I was thinking these thoughts, I was getting answers back. It was a soothing, calming male voice. It was the perfect pitch and music to my ears. He said, "He will." I asked "He will?!!" He said, "Yes." With each answer I could feel the weight of worry come off my spirit. It brought new meaning to the earth phrase of carrying the weight of the world on your shoulders. I said, "Why won't God stick up for me?" He told me, "It is all temporary, the things you are dealing with." I told him, "I didn't do all those things I was being accused of. But, no one believed me." He said, "I believe you." I said, "You do?" I can't tell you how great it felt to have someone believe me. I was still staring out at Earth. It was so close to where I was. I was in awe of the size and colors.

I went through the rest of my thoughts. "I wish I was beautiful." I heard, "You are." I said, "I am?!" He said, "Yes." I said, "Oh really? Because when I saw myself in the light, I looked the same. He said "That's not you." I said "Really?" thinking to myself I've always wanted to be more beautiful than I thought I was. I thought about what he said for a while. Happy to know that this wasn't the real me. I was just so happy someone thought I was beautiful. I was overflowing with joy with each response. Still all the while being held by someone. I said "I wish I could sing good." He said "You do." I said "Really?!" He said "Yes." I said "I wish I was perfect." He said "You are!" I said "I am?!" He said "Yes, you are."

Well, I thought I must have been doing something wrong to be abused. So I thought it was because I was a bad kid. (I wasn't) But, I said, "I didn't think I was perfect because I always got beat. I wanted to be good all the time so no one was mad at me. I seemed to always mess up and I don't want God to be mad at me." He said, "There is nothing you could do that could ever change the way God feels about you. God Loves You." I said, "He does?" He said, "Yes he does."

I said, "I wish I was special, like the people in the Bible." He said "You are." I said "Really, I am?" He said "Yes, you are." I said, "I wish God Loved me like the people in the Bible." He said "He does!" I said, "He does?" He said, "Yes HE does!" I can't tell you the feeling through all this. I wish I could download it and send it to everyone. Like every particle that is making up who you are is bursting with LOVE and Bliss. I said, "I just want to be with God. I just want to be with You!" He said, "You will!"

At this time I turned around at the sometime, I was saying "Really? I will?" There before me was the most BEAUTIFUL man I have ever seen in my whole life! The look on his face was pure LOVE and excitement. I have never ever had anyone look at me like this. His eyes wide with excitement and overflowing with LOVE and JOY. The Bluest Blue I have seen in my life. He was young, tall, dark and the most handsomest man alive. There is no living person to ever exist that could match the BEAUTY of Jesus Christ. He was perfect in every sense of the way. He ran to me and I to him. He embraced me and held me so close. I melted into him and was hooked to his side from there on out. We just got lost in each other loving gaze for a long while it seemed.

I said to Jesus, "You mean I don't have to go to sleep forever?" He kind of laughed and said "No." Jesus told me, "You will live forever and never die. This place is your HOME and always has been. You will spend eternity here."

I can't describe the feeling I felt knowing this information. On earth I was taught that I won't go to Heaven, let alone be with God or Jesus. They told me that when you die you go into like an eternal sleep state. That your body is your soul and when your body dies your soul dies and you are in this sleep state until Jesus comes to wake you up. That's what they teach anyway.

He asked me, "What would you like to do? Stay here or go back to Earth?" I said, "I didn't know what I was supposed to do there (Earth)." He told me, "Love and have fun." I said, "That's it?" I said, "I do, I love everyone." He said while smiling at me, so kind and full of love., "I know you do." He seemed to say it like he was proud of me. I was thinking to myself, "Well, no one likes me there." He said, "Yes they do." I said, "They do?" Thinking, "Well, they have a funny way of showing it." I said, "But, no one loves me." He said, "I Love you!" I said, "You do?" He held me close, holding onto my hands in front of him close to his chest. He said, "Yes, I do." We just stared into one another eyes some more. Both of us full of love for one another. I could stare at him forever and never turn my gaze.

I asked what was on Earth for me if I went back. He told me he has little presents for me strewed across this lifetime for me. He told me about all the animals that he had for me. He told me about how much they loved me. I said, "Animals can love?" He said, "Yes, of course they can!" He showed me my life in the future if I were to go back. It played out on the see-through wall that was overlooking earth. I saw myself happy and laughing so much. I wanted to be that happy because I was so unhappy while I was on earth. It is torture to be abused and growing up being told you're not going to heaven. I think my spirit was just crushed here on earth. I wanted to experience what that girl was that I watching in front of me. I saw myself get married and I was so happy to just be alive. I saw all the people I was going to save and bring to God. I just wanted everyone to feel the way I was feeling. The love was perfect and it was enough, I didn't want anything else. It was all I wanted and still all I want! After I saw how many people I was going to help bring to God. I knew I wanted to come back but, I was still scared to come back. I wasn't in a good home and I was being abused daily.

I broke my gaze with Jesus and started to look out onto Earth. I wanted him to come with me but, I thought he wouldn't come with me if I asked. The thought of him saying "no" was overwhelming to me. I thought I wasn't good enough and thought he was too beautiful to want to come back with someone like me. I said, "If I go back I don't want to stay long." He said, "okay." I prepared myself to ask if he would please come with me. I thought there is no way he is going to come with me. But, I loved him so much already. I never wanted him to leave me, ever! I turned back and looked at him. He was still smiling at me the same as he had the whole time. He expression never changed and he never took his eyes off me during the whole experience; from the time I first saw him, to when I didn't see him anymore. I thought if he came back with me, no one would hurt me. Then I can prove to my step-mother that I didn't do all the things she accused me of. He believes me and he could stick up for me. That, and he is the most beautiful man I have ever seen or will see again. I got brave and asked, "Would you please come with me?" He answered right away and said, "Sure I'll go." I ran to him and he to me and I said, "YOU WILL?!" He was still smiling at me and wide eyed with those magnificent deep Blue eyes. He held me close again with my hands in his and close to his chest. I was so happy I can't express it at all in words. We got lost in one another gaze again. Both just bursting with love. I was over the moon and overflowing with joy, love, excitement and a feeling of being in LOVE. (I still am every time I think about it)

Then this man came into the room from a door behind where we were standing. He was very beautiful with the same expression on his face as Jesus. He seemed to be super happy to see me and handed Jesus a scroll. There was a little podium next Jesus and he signed something. I looked at the man behind Jesus, and he was just smiling at me so big and loving. The man didn't stay long and left out the same door he came in. Jesus wanted me to go somewhere with him as he wanted to show me a few things. I walked with him for what seemed like a very long while. The landscaping was so perfect and everything was in bloom. It was such a magical place that the description is beyond words.

I remember walking on this path/street with Jesus and we came to a house or part of one anyway. I could the side of the house had a body of water near it. Jesus said it was a reflection pond. I was eager to check it out and went ahead of Jesus to get a better look. I turned around to see where Jesus was and he was just watching me in all my excitement. Eyes wide and full of Love for me, still smiling as big as can be. I waited for him to come closer to me and he told me "This is your house." I said, "Really, this is my house?" It was perfect and I loved it without even seeing it. We went in the house and I wanted to go right out to the reflection pond. I was debating if I really wanted to go back or not. I loved it where I was and was thinking of not going back. Jesus just watched me his expression never changing from those wide eyes and contagious smile.

We sat at the pond for a while and gazed at one another with love and affection. I just couldn't believe the house was mine, it was perfect. Jesus had something else to show me before we left to come back to Earth. Jesus and I walked for a little while, hand in hand. I am not sure where we went because I was just staring at Jesus the whole time. I remember Jesus being excited to show me something. I was eager to see what it was. I mean, he just gave me a house. No one ever did or gave me anything except my Grandma.

Jesus opened a door and when I walked in, there was a great multitude of people whose number I couldn't count. They were all smiling at me like Jesus was. So was the man in the office with the scroll. Jesus said, "All these people love you." I said, "They do?" Everyone was glowing with the colors of heaven. Full of love and light and super excited to see me. They were all telling me telepathically that they loved me and were proud of me. I wanted to stay and visit with all of them.

I loved every single one, even though I didn't know a number of how many were there. I said to Jesus, "I wish I hadn't spent so much time in the tree. I could maybe have visited with them." I felt bad for not talking to those two women before because I knew now how they all felt about me. Jesus started laughing at about the tree comment. Everyone thought it was funny and laughed. It was so magical and I will never forget it!

We had to leave and go back to earth. We all said our goodbyes. Jesus and I left all the people. Jesus had to do something before we set off together to come back. He said, "It might be a little strange or weird." I said, "Okay." The only way to describe this is like...He got into me. I could see and feel him in me. It was like I could see through his eyes and mine at the same time. After that we left HOME behind and set off back to earth. I remember it was so fast and yet I knew we traveled a great distance.

I saw a flash of light from behind me and WHOOSH we were back in space. I felt like I was ever expanding and knew where everything was. How far the planets were from me. There seemed to be no boundary that I could sense or feel. I was stopped in space above Earth. I wanted to get one last look around before I had to come back to this dirty world and this fleshly body. It felt like I was being held in someone's arms. From the moment I put my hand in the light, I was being hugged and held. But, I was facing forward sitting almost Indian style with my hand folded in my lap. I realized I wasn't breathing but, I was still alive. Jesus told me that the body needed to breath, not YOU.

Than I noticed a breeze going right through me. It was so pleasant I wanted to remember it always. I live in Florida so it's always too hot for me. I have a skin problem that makes it uncomfortable to be hot. So, the breeze was perfect temperature for me. I looked at the water of Earth and wanted to see the water. Then WHOOSH just like that we were flying so fast it was awesome. I was smiling like I have never before. Like a rollercoaster ride but, a million times better. There is no fear of heights or falling. It was a ride I will never forget. We raced down to the water and splash! The water was parting like the red sea, but on a much smaller scale. I wasn't getting wet and I was in a sphere. I thought, "Oh what a shame, I am not getting wet. I liked the feeling of water on my skin." Jesus said, "Your body gets wet not you." I was a little bummed, but nothing major.

I was skimming across the top of the water and laughed as we flew away back to the hospital. I took one last look around before going back in this body. I thought, "Eewww, it's heavy and dirty, hot and sweaty." I didn't have any attachment to it at all. I was grossed out by it to be honest. I said, "Where do I go in?" I was trying to get back into my body. Right then, I easily went right in. I entered at the bottom of the sternum area. It was so weird being in the body. It felt more like a hollow shell on the inside and dense on the outside. I didn't know what to do when I re-entered this fleshly body. I bounced around on the inside for a few seconds. I moved down the legs and back up the legs. Down the arms and back up the arms. I started to hear the people trying to wake me up. I couldn't talk or reconnect to this body. Jesus said, "It will take just a second to reconnect with your body." I thought, "Okay, I will just stay in my head until I can answer." Finally I said, "Does anyone have a breath mint?" They told me I couldn't have anything, not even water. Ice chips were the only thing I could have. I thought my breath was pretty bad. So, I thought about every mint, gum and mouth wash I could remember. The medical staff was pretty annoyed with me. I didn't want to have bad breath and answer questions with them in my face. I got taken to my hospital room where my Father was waiting for me. I was looking around for Jesus and I didn't see him. I thought for sure he would walk right through the door.

It took me almost a year to learn how to walk again. My life changed after this happened. I am forever changed by the love Jesus showed to me.

What I later learned and felt as I grew up, was that Jesus was inside of me. He was a part of me. Although I kept expecting him to appear, he only did this once since my NDE. But, as much as a fourteen year old wants to be vindicated and protected against abuse, I would not have grown as much if Jesus had appeared. The spirituality that I share with Jesus and the remembrance of that indescribable, unconditional love is what carries me through in life.

I did meet my soulmate. We have been married for two years now. And as I was shown – I have a wonderful, loving life and I have a solid support system with my friends. Life is now fun.

At the time of your experience was there an associated life-threatening event? Yes.

Was the experience difficult to express in words? Yes. It's very difficult to express in words because the experience was more than words could ever describe. It's something there are no words for. You don't have a point of reference in your mind to refer to. You can't download the feelings of the experience. No words could touch the experience I had.

At what time during the experience were you at your highest level of consciousness and alertness? More consciousness and alertness than normal. Pretty much the whole experience was that way. From the time I left this body, to the time I re-entered this body. This was highest level of possible consciousness I have ever had in my entire life before or since. I was out of this fleshly body for the entire experience, from the time I popped out to the time I re-entered.

Please compare your vision during the experience to your everyday vision that you had immediately prior to the time of the experience. One couldn't compare the two at all. I was doing more than seeing with earthly eyes. I was seeing it and feeling with my soul in all it's perfection. The colors are so much brighter and full of light and more colors in the spectrum than in this fleshly body. As soon as I could see out of these earthly eyes it was all so different. Colors were more muted and the color spectrum went back to what we are used to.

Please compare your hearing during the experience to your everyday hearing that you had immediately prior to the time of the experience. One can't compare the two at all. I was doing more than hearing with my earthly ears. I was hearing it and feeling it with my soul in all it's perfection. I this fleshly body I can't hear well at one ear and I get infections easily. When I re-entered this fleshly body I could hear Jesus still talking to me. But, it was with my soul not my earthly ears.

Did you see or hear any earthly events that were occurring during a time that your consciousness/awareness was apart from your physical/earthly body? Yes. When I left this fleshly body I just heard some surgical instruments being used. It was super deafening and very high pitched. When I came back and re-entered this fleshly body I heard the surgical staff talking to me, trying to get me to wake up.

What emotions did you feel during the experience? Perfect Love, bliss, ecstasy, elation, passion and excitement of being IN LOVE. I also felt immense acceptance.

Did you pass into or through a tunnel? No.

Did you see an unearthly light? Yes. I was in the void I guess you'd call it. It was blacker than the blackest I have ever seen. I was scared of the dark thinking something was going to get me. I was scared of the dark on earth. I expressed my fear of the dark and wondered where was the light was? Immediately I saw I pin prick of light and WHOOSH it was coming at me so fast I like jumped out of the way because I thought I was going to be hit. I put my hand in it and it felt so amazing and was loving me. It seemed to be alive and lavishing me with affection and holding me close and tight. I never wanted to leave from it. I danced in it and spun around over and over. I wanted to remember it forever, that feeling of perfect love!

Did you seem to encounter a mystical being or presence, or hear an unidentifiable voice? I encountered a definite being, or a voice clearly of mystical or unearthly origin. I saw two white light beings that greeted me at the lights. They were more of than bodies or detailed in anyway. I saw two women walking on a street/path. they were young and beautiful and wearing bright white dresses. The dresses were simple almost looked like white wool or something. They wore like a belt or tie around the waists. I saw a very handsome man with a scroll and he smiled at me with such love and excitement.

Did you encounter or become aware of any deceased (or alive) beings? Yes. Jesus, My beloved, my first LOVE.

Did you become aware of past events in your life during your experience? No.

Did you seem to enter some other, unearthly world? A clearly mystical or unearthly realm. It was like a boundary or border of clouds. I watched myself go through these clouds as if I wasn't in control of anything. I came to a world of LIGHTS! There was no darkness at ALL! Everything was like clear gold and sparkly. The Colors were so magnificent. I wanted to look at the flowers and WHOOSH there they were BOOM right in front of me like I was looking at them through a microscope. I walked a path or street that was like clear gold. Everything was so perfect in every sense of the way. The landscaping was pristine!! Everything was in bloom and alive with light. There were no dead leaves or twigs on any of the plants, trees and flowers. There was no source of light anywhere. Everything was super bright and light was everywhere. I walked along a path or street and I came to a fork in the road and a huge building. The building was so amazing in it's design. It appeared to be in the ground and apart of the ground. There was 12, like crystal foundations (it's the only thing I can liken it too) There were names written on them in different colors.

Did time seem to speed up or slow down? Everything seemed to be happening at once; or time stopped or lost all meaning. There was no sense of time really.

Did you suddenly seem to understand everything? No.

Did you reach a boundary or limiting physical structure? No.

Did you come to a border or point of no return? No.

Did scenes from the future come to you? Scenes from my personal future, I saw my life play out before me. I also saw my future played out before me.

Did you have a sense of knowing special knowledge or purpose? Yes. Love; that is it.

Discuss any changes that might have occurred in your life after your experience. Slight changes in my life. I left that religion and never looked back. I won't allow myself to be limited in soul development because of someone else's interpretation of what I already know to be true. I don't judge anyone for any reason at all. I was told to LOVE and that is what I am going to do.

Did you have any changes in your values or beliefs after the experience that occurred as a result of the experience? Yes. I loved everything and everyone when I came back. Even if they didn't like me I still cared for them. Trees, animals and everything living I took another look at. They are living and loving us and we don't even realize it. I no longer go to church nor am I a member of any organized religion. It brought me closer to Jesus whom I didn't really personally know before.

Do you have any psychic, non-ordinary or other special gifts after your experience that you did not have before the experience? Uncertain. I have always had special gifts that I had to keep quiet due to religious persecution and public shunning. So I kept it to myself for over 20 years. Now, I do Tarot Card readings and can see things before they happen. I am still trying to figure out what these gifts are. But, after the experience I would say I wasn't afraid to use my gift.

Have you ever shared this experience with others? Yes. I have told a handful of friends and I have told my husband and Mother. My husband thinks it's amazing and it's taught him a lot. I told a few friends and some believe me and other don't believe me. But, love me enough to hear it out and talk about it. Even though they don't believe in God or much of anything like that. When I told my Mother it was hard because she is still on the old belief systems I let go so long ago. So, it's too much to get her mind around. In one breath, my mother doesn't believe me, but in the next breath, she is supportive.. So, people are all over the spectrum.

Did you have any knowledge of near death experience (NDE) prior to your experience? No.

What did you believe about the reality of your experience shortly (days to weeks) after it happened? Experience was definitely real. It was more real than this life or anything I've ever experienced.

What do you believe about the reality of your experience at the current time? Experience was definitely real. It's more real and vivid than anything else I have ever experienced. And no one can take that away from me.

Have your relationships changed specifically as a result of your experience? No.

Have your religious beliefs/spiritual practices changed specifically as a result of your experience? Yes.

At any time in your life, has anything ever reproduced any part of the experience? No.

Did the questions asked and information that you provided accurately and comprehensively describe your experience? Yes.

Are there one or several parts of your experience that are especially meaningful or significant to you? There were some personal things Jesus and I talked about that involved my life. They way he loves me and looks at me make me melt. I think the whole experience was meaningful and significant to me. I think it would be to hard to pick a few that stand out more. When the experience is made to be so personal and touching to you personally. When Jesus told me I was going to be with God forever and that he loved me. I am forever changed by his love for me.

Is there anything else that you would like to add about your experience? I can't wait to go HOME! There is a place for everyone and that LOVE doesn't just happen to me, it happens to all of us. It's so incredible I want everyone to know him and know that LOVE!

CONCLUSION

All of the NDErs responded so lovingly to the request to put their experiences in a format so that people who do not have access to a computer, who are elderly, or who are handicapped could be inspired and comforted by these wonderful experiences. One of the questions that we ask is, if NDEs are for the experiencer or for the world? The answer is "both." You've been able to read about how remarkable these experiences are and what profound effects they have had on NDErs. I'm here to tell you that after 14 years of reading NDEs, that these stories have profoundly affected our readers too. One of the biggest areas it has affected readers is how they view death. Emotions range from curiosity to relief. The fact that a person is immortal changes the choices they make on earth. A person consciously chooses to live their lives differently. Many who are grieving or worried about what the afterlife contains for themselves or a loved one are able to forgive themselves and spend more time with the people they love in their lives. People learn that death is nothing to be feared.

Other themes that are part of the NDEs is reincarnation, judgment, religion, lessons, universal purpose, light beings, communication, and of course LOVE! Since the soul is immortal, it is not unthinkable that the soul existed before this incarnation or will exist after death. The NDEs confirm that these souls lived before and that they live again. God sees only love when the judgment occurs. It is used as a learning tool for the individual to help them spiritually grow. There is no condemnation.

Interestingly, another tenet of religions is that many claim that they are the only way to God. Yet, through the NDE wisdom, there are many paths to God like many paths up to the top of a mountain. Each person has a choice and an important part to play in his or her spiritual growth. Families come together to create the setting for particular lessons and missions on earth. Our guides are typically light beings, because we on earth are also light beings and we are interconnected with them.

The concept of unity and interconnectedness is all part of the universal matrix. We communicate on the other sided through thought/feeling. Everybody is part of this universal matrix. Even though they are individuals, by being interconnected, they are a part of each other and can hear, think, and feel all at the same time. The environment is pure love, so there is nothing but peace and harmony as everyone communicates with everyone else.

Learning about universal, unconditional love, is probably better imagined than described. But the NDErs whose stories you read, did a tremendous job at trying to explain this aspect. The biggest way that knowledge of unconditional love affects people is the way that people treat themselves and others around them. When they realize that love is all there is and that is what we are judged on when we go to the other side, our priorities on earth change. We treat people with love, compassion, tolerance, patience – all the qualities that embody unconditional love. It would be wonderful if everyone could read NDEs!

It is also important to understand that NDEs are a global phenomenon. We have NDEs from people all over the world, different ages, different cultures, and different religions. If more people could understand how the universe really works and about the unconditional love from where we originate from, then we could truly become a heaven on earth. We could create a golden age where humans can live in love, peace and harmony.

Paperbacks also available from
White Crow Books

Elsa Barker—*Letters from
a Living Dead Man*
ISBN 978-1-907355-83-7

Elsa Barker—*War Letters from
the Living Dead Man*
ISBN 978-1-907355-85-1

Elsa Barker—*Last Letters from
the Living Dead Man*
ISBN 978-1-907355-87-5

Richard Maurice Bucke—
Cosmic Consciousness
ISBN 978-1-907355-10-3

Arthur Conan Doyle—
The Edge of the Unknown
ISBN 978-1-907355-14-1

Arthur Conan Doyle—
The New Revelation
ISBN 978-1-907355-12-7

Arthur Conan Doyle—
The Vital Message
ISBN 978-1-907355-13-4

Arthur Conan Doyle with
Simon Parke—*Conversations
with Arthur Conan Doyle*
ISBN 978-1-907355-80-6

Meister Eckhart with Simon Parke—
Conversations with Meister Eckhart
ISBN 978-1-907355-18-9

D. D. Home—*Incidents in my Life Part 1*
ISBN 978-1-907355-15-8

Mme. Dunglas Home; edited,
with an Introduction, by Sir
Arthur Conan Doyle—*D. D.
Home: His Life and Mission*
ISBN 978-1-907355-16-5

Edward C. Randall—
Frontiers of the Afterlife
ISBN 978-1-907355-30-1

Rebecca Ruter Springer—
Intra Muros: My Dream of Heaven
ISBN 978-1-907355-11-0

Leo Tolstoy, edited by Simon
Parke—*Forbidden Words*
ISBN 978-1-907355-00-4

Leo Tolstoy—*A Confession*
ISBN 978-1-907355-24-0

Leo Tolstoy—*The Gospel in Brief*
ISBN 978-1-907355-22-6

Leo Tolstoy—*The Kingdom
of God is Within You*
ISBN 978-1-907355-27-1

Leo Tolstoy—*My Religion:
What I Believe*
ISBN 978-1-907355-23-3

Leo Tolstoy—*On Life*
ISBN 978-1-907355-91-2

Leo Tolstoy—*Twenty-three Tales*
ISBN 978-1-907355-29-5

Leo Tolstoy—*What is Religion
and other writings*
ISBN 978-1-907355-28-8

Leo Tolstoy—*Work While
Ye Have the Light*
ISBN 978-1-907355-26-4

Leo Tolstoy—*The Death of Ivan Ilyich*
ISBN 978-1-907661-10-5

Leo Tolstoy—*Resurrection*
ISBN 978-1-907661-09-9

Leo Tolstoy with Simon Parke—
Conversations with Tolstoy
ISBN 978-1-907355-25-7

Howard Williams with an Introduction
by Leo Tolstoy—*The Ethics of Diet:
An Anthology of Vegetarian Thought*
ISBN 978-1-907355-21-9

Vincent Van Gogh with Simon
Parke—*Conversations with Van Gogh*
ISBN 978-1-907355-95-0

Wolfgang Amadeus Mozart with Simon
Parke—*Conversations with Mozart*
ISBN 978-1-907661-38-9

Jesus of Nazareth with Simon Parke—
Conversations with Jesus of Nazareth
ISBN 978-1-907661-41-9

Thomas à Kempis with Simon
Parke—*The Imitation of Christ*
ISBN 978-1-907661-58-7

Julian of Norwich with Simon
Parke—*Revelations of Divine Love*
ISBN 978-1-907661-88-4

Allan Kardec—*The Spirits Book*
ISBN 978-1-907355-98-1

Allan Kardec—*The Book on Mediums*
ISBN 978-1-907661-75-4

Emanuel Swedenborg—*Heaven and Hell*
ISBN 978-1-907661-55-6

P.D. Ouspensky—*Tertium Organum:
The Third Canon of Thought*
ISBN 978-1-907661-47-1

Dwight Goddard—*A Buddhist Bible*
ISBN 978-1-907661-44-0

Michael Tymn—*The Afterlife Revealed*
ISBN 978-1-970661-90-7

Michael Tymn—*Transcending the
Titanic: Beyond Death's Door*
ISBN 978-1-908733-02-3

Guy L. Playfair—*If This Be Magic*
ISBN 978-1-907661-84-6

Guy L. Playfair—*The Flying Cow*
ISBN 978-1-907661-94-5

Guy L. Playfair —*This House is Haunted*
ISBN 978-1-907661-78-5

Carl Wickland, M.D.—
Thirty Years Among the Dead
ISBN 978-1-907661-72-3

John E. Mack—*Passport to the Cosmos*
ISBN 978-1-907661-81-5

Peter & Elizabeth Fenwick—
The Truth in the Light
ISBN 978-1-908733-08-5

Erlendur Haraldsson—
Modern Miracles
ISBN 978-1-908733-25-2

Erlendur Haraldsson—
At the Hour of Death
ISBN 978-1-908733-27-6

Erlendur Haraldsson—
The Departed Among the Living
ISBN 978-1-908733-29-0

Brian Inglis—*Science and Parascience*
ISBN 978-1-908733-18-4

Brian Inglis—*Natural and Supernatural:
A History of the Paranormal*
ISBN 978-1-908733-20-7

Ernest Holmes—*The Science of Mind*
ISBN 978-1-908733-10-8

Victor & Wendy Zammit —*A Lawyer
Presents the Evidence For the Afterlife*
ISBN 978-1-908733-22-1

Casper S. Yost—*Patience
Worth: A Psychic Mystery*
ISBN 978-1-908733-06-1

William Usborne Moore—
Glimpses of the Next State
ISBN 978-1-907661-01-3

William Usborne Moore—
The Voices
ISBN 978-1-908733-04-7

John W. White—
The Highest State of Consciousness
ISBN 978-1-908733-31-3

Stafford Betty—
The Imprisoned Splendor
ISBN 978-1-907661-98-3

Paul Pearsall, Ph.D. —
Super Joy
ISBN 978-1-908733-16-0

**All titles available as eBooks, and selected titles available in Hardback and
Audiobook formats from www.whitecrowbooks.com**

CPSIA information can be obtained at www.ICGtesting.com
Printed in the USA
LVOW13s0416020514

384175LV00004B/445/P